D1707043

A Reading of
MANSFIELD PARK

An Essay in Critical Synthesis

by

AVROM FLEISHMAN

THE JOHNS HOPKINS PRESS
Baltimore and London

Copyright © 1967 by the University of Minnesota
All rights reserved
Manufactured in the United States of America

The Johns Hopkins Press, Baltimore, Maryland 21218
The Johns Hopkins Press Ltd., London

Standard Book Number 8018-1149-x

Johns Hopkins Paperbacks edition, 1970

Original edition published by the University of Minnesota
Press, Minneapolis, Minnesota, from whom a clothbound
edition is available.

The quotation from Clarence Branton on pages 87–88 is © 1955 by
The Regents of the University of California. Reprinted from
Nineteenth-Century Fiction, X, 156–159, by permission of The
Regents and Mr. Branton. Portions of Chapter III appeared in
Nineteenth-Century Fiction, June 1967.

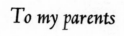

To my parents

To my parents

Preface

As ITS title suggests, this study proposes to be experimental in method as well as exhaustive of its subject. It aims at a unified and full reading of a novel, and proposes Jane Austen's *Mansfield Park* as example. The method, having nothing new in its elements, is to apply a variety of critical approaches instead of choosing one or another of them, for applied in isolation they have led to misunderstandings of the novel. By widening the range of points of view, one makes it possible to see the novel as a subtle response to its own age and to certain eternal human concerns, rather than as the narrow defense of outworn values it has been taken to be.

Although the theoretical and practical reasons for the multi-perspectival criticism here attempted are set out in an introductory chapter, it must be confessed that these studies have, in their first forms, not been written according to a program. Since my first study of the novel as an undergraduate in Lionel Trilling's courses, I have tried at various points in my career as student and teacher to write on *Mansfield Park*, and each time have felt it necessary to start afresh. Yet the discarded studies have always seemed to me to retain a partial validity: each time, the approach of the moment seemed to offer thorough comprehension, but became in its turn as conditional as the others. I have reached my critical pluralism the hard way, becoming convinced that no single point of view can be commensurate with the manifold reality of a great novel and that only the joining of minds — or of one's own mind in its changing forms — can achieve a comprehensive view.

Almost every year of late has seen an excellent article on *Mansfield Park* to which the reader's response must be: very true, as far as it goes.[1] I have tried to go on somewhat longer than most studies of individual novels, in the hope of going somewhat further. But I should have learned nothing from experience if I did not anticipate the response — perhaps my own in future — that this, too, is by no means the whole story. In any case, my employment of still tendentious sociological, pyschological, and anthropological theories insures that no reader will be equally acquiescent to all parts of this study.

In the course of a long preparation for the writing of this monograph, I have had the direct and indirect benefits of association with the following teachers, some of whom were also my colleagues: Earl R. Wasserman, J. Hillis Miller, Leonard Unger, Robert E. Moore, Roy Arthur Swanson, and Harry R. Hoppe. If I have differed with some of them in conversation or in writing, my work has always been the better for the dialogue.

Table of Contents

A READING OF *MANSFIELD PARK*

"Here begins the village. Those cottages are really a disgrace. The church spire is reckoned remarkably handsome. I am glad the church is not so close to the Great House as often happens in old places. The annoyance of the bells must be terrible. There is the parsonage; a tidy looking house, and I understand the clergyman and his wife are very decent people. Those are alms-houses, built by some of the family. To the right is the steward's house; he is a very respectable man. Now we are coming to the lodge gates; but we have nearly a mile through the park still. It is not ugly, you see, at this end; there is some fine timber, but the situation of the house is dreadful. . . ."

from Maria Bertram's description of Sotherton Court

I

Introduction: The Whole Novel

OF HOW many subjects of literary study can it be observed that where once articles were to be written, today only books will do. The weight of accumulated evidence on such transcendent works as *The Canterbury Tales, Paradise Lost,* or almost any of Shakespeare's plays has led to an increasing number of full-length studies that incorporate a variety of sources of information to exhaust separate aspects of each work. Furthering the movement in this direction is the pervasiveness of the new-critical approach, which isolates the individual work of art as the proper scope of study. But the principal motive, it would seem, is the sheer complexity of the available scholarship, which makes it well-nigh impossible to say anything authoritative about a major work without taking account of all that is known about it.

This embarrassment of riches is particularly acute in the criticism of fiction. In the field of modern fiction, especially, the wave of studies of certain novels has become almost tidal. *A Portrait of the Artist as a Young Man,* "Heart of Darkness," *The Great Gatsby* — to name some current favorites — have been inundated by articles devoted exclusively to them. This persistence may be due to the great popularity, relative simplicity, or mere availability of modern fiction in general or of these novels in particular, but whatever the reason the result is to leave a mass of information unsynthesized and sterile, while an apparently endless multiplication of effort proceeds unchecked. The pressing need — and the golden opportunity — in the criticism of fiction is for extended studies of individual works about which enough is known to permit an approximation to a total reading.

The synthesis of available research on major texts is not only a temporary desideratum, brought on by the needs of the moment in the history of literary scholarship; it also has certain theoretical advantages to recommend it. Organic structure, which the new criticism has made a commonplace by its focus on lyric poetry, has been discovered to be the condition as much of great long poems as of short ones. Despite occasional reaffirmations of Poe's "poetic principle" of lyric intensity at the expense of epic amplitude, modern criticism has found that certain long works have a unity as binding as that of lyrics. Recent readings of long poems like *King Lear, The Faerie Queene,* and *The Prelude* have established their high degree of integration of thematic, verbal, and symbolic elements. If such poems are to be read organically, the systematic and sustained monograph promises to become the normal critical form.

What is true for the long poem holds for the novel as well, but it does not hold in quite the same way. For the novel, the appropriate methodology is not the same as that for a poem, whose organic unity requires on principle that it be read as a whole. It is rather the peculiar diversity of the novel that encourages a variety of points of view and forces us to enlarge the scope of criticism. It is, indeed, possible to make a metaphysical virtue of this practical necessity. Many contemporary philosophers, of whom Ortega y Gasset is the most prominent, have shown that experiential truth is approachable not from any one of our limited human perspectives but only by the harmonious union of a variety of perspectives.[1] The novel, Ortega also maintains, is an impure, dense, and textured form; it contains in loose suspension the stuff of experience, establishing an "inner world" as manifold as the "outer reality." To deal with this heterogeneous experience the critic needs the same kind of perspectival flexibility as the observer of complex scientific phenomena, who must take account of the special conditions of each observation and then induce into these partial, "subjective" points of view a hypothetical — but never personally experienced — objective one.

The critical implication of the perspectival view of the novel is to consider it an organic diversity. It is organic in the degree to which its multitudinousness creates the illusion of a living world; the escape of many fictional details from any critical net cast to hold them can substantiate an impression of life's heterogeneity. If the novel is by nature various, our points of view on it must follow suit. How these divergent points of view are integrated is akin to the process that integrates our lived experience: we add perspective to perspective, the lights of each illuminating the dark corners of the other, until a sense of reality is adumbrated.

These preliminary remarks will probably win more general assent than any enumeration of the perspectives to be employed. Despite a widespread awareness that we are living in the age of Freud and Marx (it has even been suggested that these names be used without capitals, to show that they signify no longer merely persons but primary elements of modern intellectual life), there is still a pervasive distrust of Freudianism and Marxism in themselves and especially in their application to literature. That they are distrusted as such is natural enough in the light of their real or supposed threat to traditional political and religious institutions. That they are distrusted in their application to literature is possibly to be accounted to their tendency to usurp the traditional authority of purely literary criticism, instead of humbly serving to inform it with the data of social-scientific observation. Yet they must be included if criticism is to have a claim to comprehensiveness.

The subject matter of the realistic novel — the interaction of society and personality — has, since its great age in the nineteenth-century, become the object of scientific, or at least purportedly scientific, investigation by nonliterary disciplines: the novelist is no longer the sole interpreter of personal behavior in a social milieu. Because the literary and the more or less scientific views over-lap, there is much to be gained and much to be wary of in bringing them together. Ideally, the partial perspective of each would be strengthened as it complements the others. In practice, this cor-relation turns into a narrowing of view which may be called re-ductionism. Sociologically and psychologically oriented critics have often taken up the habits of the professionals of those disci-plines, and have tended to substitute the scientific fact for the im-aginative interpretation of literature. They forget, or do not be-lieve, that the object of literary study is to discover how the raw materials of art are transmuted into something more powerful and beautiful than the elements in which they began. Instead, most psychologists and sociologists of literature work backward, trans-muting artistic creation back into primal chaos. Criticism must keep as its end the elucidation of the whole work of art, in which each partial perspective points toward a higher unity.

In the chapters that follow, scientific (even, perhaps, pseudo-scientific) information will be used unabashedly, in the hope of illuminating separate aspects of *Mansfield Park* and in the expecta-tion that a combination of these partial views will overcome local distortions. To put the matter in the words of Ortega's "Notes on the Novel": "*Within* the novel almost anything fits: science, re-ligion, sociology, aesthetic criticism — if only it is ultimately de-realized and confined within the inner world of the novel; i.e., if it remains without actual and effective validity. In other words, a novel can contain as much sociology as it desires, but the novel it-self cannot be sociological." [2] Though this aesthetic may not be fully adequate to a view of the novelist's function, it suggests an apt formula for the critic's. Criticism can contain as much socio-logical data as it needs to explain the "derealized" social observa-tion in the novel, but it must not itself become sociological, pre-tending to scientific objectivity. Only the sum of error-laden per-spectives can approach the truth, in our relativist, heterogeneous, complex universe or in its truest fictions.

Historical fact has also at times been used reductively by schol-ars who wish to limit the content of literature to the historical situ-

ations it reflects. Surely this enterprise presupposes an unsophisti-
cated notion of what constitutes historical fact — a notion which
may quickly be modified by a reading of R. G. Collingwood's *The
Idea of History*. Fact is what weighers of evidence believe to be
true, and historical fact is especially bound up with what prior re-
searchers believed to be true. Historical fact has, therefore, an imaginative character and invites us to put ourselves back in time, to
feel the evocative power of the novel's reflected facts over the imagination of the author's contemporaries. A novel has a number of
historical halos of significance which arrange themselves around
the facts in the text: first for the characters at the time of the action,
then for the author's contemporaries, and finally for the modern
reader in the light of recent knowledge. The "historical" critic must
therefore be at least as imaginative as the "new"; he, too, is dealing
with the subjective process of meaning when he deals with the impact of the novel's facts on its various audiences. A case in point is
presented by *Mansfield Park*. The novel makes little explicit reference to the economic situation of Antigua — although it was written in the wake of the Abolition Act — yet these important colonial
associations would have been in the mind of any reasonably well-
informed reader of the time. Neither the characters in the novel
nor modern readers are much struck by the historical facts, but
the historical critic must reveal their significance to the immediate
audience — without claiming, of course, to have exhausted the novel's meaning.

It seems to have been Jane Austen's assumption that the novel,
to reverse Ortega's formula, may be sociological, but must contain
no sociology: it may trace the impact of historical reality on fictional subjects, or make special appeals to the contemporary imagination, but it must not import data into the text itself. As a result of
this rigorous artistic control of her materials, Jane Austen has become the novelist we lean on most heavily to tell us what it was like
to be alive in England at the beginning of the nineteenth century,
yet in whose works we can discover no documentation of the period. We are, for example, never asked to think of Fanny Price as
a war victim, yet such she is, her family's poverty being the result

of her father's incapacitation — presumably during the Napoleonic wars. In order to win the largest perception of the world of such novels, we must bring to them not only the modern consciousness, armed with the data of the sciences, but also the kind of unspoken — not unconscious — awareness of the historical context that could be assumed of any regular reader of a contemporary newspaper. This procedure is an application in the historical realm of the perspectival method outlined above: just as the fusion of critical approaches allows a broad modern view of the novel, the union of the modern with the contemporary reader's sense of the novel can approximate a perspective unlimited by history. It is from such a point of view that we are best able to appreciate what is eternally human in the concrete and confined world of *Mansfield Park*.

II

A Novel among the Critics

ALL the doctrines expressed by the Church of England were true to him, and every word written by Jane Austen he believed to be almost as necessary to salvation. . . . he felt for those who had never known the loving kindness of the Church, and he shook his head compassionately over those who had not read *Mansfield Park*." In these words (from his novel *Unclay*), T. F. Powys immortalized a common breed of Austen reader (Kipling named them "Janeites" — faintly recalling the anachronistic Jacobites). What has attracted generations of comfortable English matrons, clergymen, antiquarians — in general, those retired from modern life — to her novels is more than a set of religious, social, or political values. Her appeal is to the need for retirement itself: whatever it is she does, she does it while maintaining for some the illusion that nothing is happening in the rest of the world — that nothing *can* happen in the world to change things very much. As a popular handbook writer put its, "The basis of Jane's work is serenity."

If this were truly the basis, nothing could be better calculated to put a writer out of critical favor in our time of troubles. Even those seeking escape from the time could hardly fail to sense the unreality or distance of such an unbeclouded world. The time in which her novels appeared was one of troubles, too, and yet her earliest readers seem not to have used her for escape. One of her contemporaries, describing *Mansfield Park*, expresses her response with a ring of finality equal to that of the passage quoted above: "It has not however that elevation of virtue, something beyond nature, that gives the greatest charm to a novel, but still it is real natural every day life." [1] Everyday life without the charm of elevated virtue: this might stand as a preliminary definition of the realistic — even of the naturalistic — novel. That there have been, from the first, readers with this acute sense of reality goes far to account for the persistence of Jane Austen.

It was, however, inevitable that she should suffer the abuse lavished on the Victorians and other parental figures by the generation decimated in World War I. Jane Austen did not incur her Lytton Strachey, but she did achieve her H. W. Garrod, who, in the year just before the great depression, wrote a formal essay in depreciation. Referring to *Mansfield Park* and its heroine, Garrod set the tone for a long series of entertaining asperities: "I daresay there is a land of promise in which we may one day meet such young women as Fanny Price . . . but it will be a land flowing with milk and water." [2] Since then it has been widely assumed that *Mansfield Park* is, in the phrase of another commentator, "Jane Austen's Victorian novel" [3] — with all the innuendo somehow still attached to that adjective.

As a supposed spokesman for the ruling class, Jane Austen was readily transformed into a symbol (or symptom) by the post-war trend toward sociological criticism. Studies with such titles as "The Economic Determinism of Jane Austen" and "Jane Austen, Karl Marx, and the Aristocratic Dance" [4] have made the social criticism in her novels a commonplace. They attempted to show the gritty reality in her description of society, and particularly her concern for the hard facts of money, class, and the marriage market. But these critics have been troubled by misgivings about the author's own attitude toward those facts and toward her society's values. Was she simply reflecting the prevailing social and economic constraints on individual freedom; was she defending or attacking the class system which enforced those constraints?

The latest Austen critics have entertained no such doubts and have decided boldly that she was a reactionary. Supposedly tough-minded critics tend to evaluate her social vision by their own political standards and find her wanting in severity toward the so-called aristocracy in her novels. It was Marvin Mudrick who brought to a high pitch the accusations against her political conservatism, and more recently Kingsley Amis has denounced her as a pillar of the Establishment.[5] The angry young critics claim superiority to Jane Austen's "going-through-the-motions appreciators" but they are themselves going-through-the-motions detractors, who remain indifferent to the complex social relations portrayed in the novels — such as the antagonism between aristocracy and gentry which pervades them. For them, "genteel" and "conventional" are pejoratives with a present-day application, rather than historical descriptions of the society in which the novels are set.

As a result of these unhistorical judgments of the novels' values, literary evaluation itself has become confused. Because the prevailing view of *Mansfield Park* assumes it to be conservative, its style is taken to be the expression of a crusty Tory. Andrew H. Wright sums up the general view: "The strict (and rather narrow) moralizing tone of *Mansfield Park* stems in part from the frequent indirect comment by the author."[6] Yet a subtler view of style is given us by a critic who has clearly seen that Jane Austen's tone reflects not her own intrusion but the dramatic situation of the novel. Mary Lascelles writes:

. . . in *Mansfield Park* Jane Austen's style develops a new faculty, out of one perceptible in all her novels — a faculty I can only describe as chameleon-like. In *Sense and Sensibility* and *Pride and Prejudice* she had shown that she could make her characters think each in his or her own idiom . . . In *Mansfield Park*, however, the habits of expression of the characters impress themselves on the narrative style of the episodes in which they are involved, and on the description of their situations. The very arrival of the Bertrams' party in the midst of the solemn grandeur of Sotherton seems to fasten weights on the style: "Mr. Rushworth was at the door to receive his fair lady, and the whole party were welcomed by him with due attention. . . . After the business of arriving was over, it was first necessary to eat, and the doors were thrown open to admit them through one or two intermediate rooms into the appointed dining-parlour, where a collation was prepared with abundance and elegance." [7]

Lacking Mary Lascelles' sense of the dramatic effect of style, critics are betrayed into judging it by current standards of taste. Here again, as in the political judgments described above, the question of historical criteria for criticism is raised.

The most important attempt to read *Mansfield Park* in broad social terms is the much reprinted essay by Lionel Trilling, which has become the standard reference to the novel. Trilling takes a historical perspective in order to defend the novel against the value judgments of liberal critics, but he does not remain content to read it in the context of its time. Rather he goes on to argue the relevance to *our* time of the author's purported views: her moral suspicion of the theater, her preference for fine country houses to lower-middle-class disorder, her desire for Neoclassic stasis rather than Romantic dynamism in life, her choice of a sickly but saintly heroine over a vivacious, amoral one. Trilling finds the novel a critique of the open society, a reaction against the idealization of individual personality that was encouraged by Romanticism and is still maintained by contemporary liberals. The burden of the essay is to recommend this challenge to fundamental assumptions as salutary self-criticism for the men of our own day.

Trilling's argument *ad hominem* often vitiates his desired historicism, however, for in attempting to win us over to the values of Jane Austen's era he is led to draw support from analogies somewhat off the mark — like the Platonic theory of art or the Victorian sense of duty. Some of these themes run through Western culture as a whole, to be sure, but we need to know how they operated at the time Jane Austen wrote. When these special forms are discovered, their application to our own time will unfortunately, but inevitably, grow less marked. We do not need to take *Mansfield Park* as a dated and irrelevant artifact of a past age; neither shall we be able to recommend it as a corrective for modern cultural tastes.

Beyond the problems of applying the values of the past to the needs of the present, there is some doubt about the specific neo-conservative lessons that are drawn from the novel. Trilling contends that "no other great novel has so anxiously asserted the need to find security, to establish, in fixity and enclosure, a refuge from the dangers of openness and chance." [8] I shall try to show that the novel, though it makes us aware of some of the dangers of modern social life, is an affirmation of a dynamic culture and a denial of the ideal of isolation; that it stands for intense social engagement, and not for a retreat from life; that its very subject is the misery that isolation brings, and its plea a plea for connection.

In the cases where historical evidence has been amply brought to bear on the political meaning of Jane Austen's novels, further refinement in its interpretation is called for. Donald J. Greene, one of the more knowing historical critics, has suggested that by indirect techniques such as the choice of the characters' names, the Tory politics of the Austen household covertly enters the novels. [9] Further, he proposes that the novels all take for their subject the clash of the rising middle class with the established aristocracy. Bennets and Darcy-DeBurghs, Elliots and Wentworths, Morlands and Tilneys, Dashwoods and Ferrars — the crux of each novel lies consistently in the problem of marriage across class lines, lines that are becoming always more fluid and yet remain resistant. "Possibly it is in *Mansfield Park*," Greene continues, "that Jane Austen comes as close as she ever does to a thoroughgoing presentation of a theory of Tory democracy, when Fanny and William Price, from an incurably lower-middle-class home, . . . 'make good' and the high-bred Maria Bertram is disgraced."

Greene's thesis has the virtue of placing Jane Austen in the mainstream of modern novelists from Defoe to Hardy whose major theme is the emergence of the bourgeoisie and its struggle with the landed classes for power and prestige. But, while the bourgeois-aristocratic marriage market is frequently scrutinized in the Austen canon, it does not exactly define the conflict of classes in *Mans-*

field Park, for the Prices are not a successful bourgeois family striving for dominance, nor are the Bertrams an aristocratic house fighting off interlopers. The titled Bertrams in fact welcome intermarriage with the Rushworths and Crawfords, of landed but not titled origins, but they are averse to one daughter's marriage to a genuine aristocrat, Mr. Yates. We shall come to see, further, that culturally and socially the Crawfords are closer to the aristocracy than to the gentry, and that this worsens rather than improves their chances of marriage with the Bertrams, who are of the gentry. The class struggle in these novels must be read with subtler distinctions than those suggested by "bourgeoisie" and "aristocracy." (See the Appendix to Chapter III.)

The most sociologically sophisticated attempt to evaluate Jane Austen's social burden has been made by Arnold Kettle, yet it is in his work that the need for greater historical specificity and terminological precision is most in evidence. Kettle wishes to salvage the Austen canon from the Marxist "philistines," who reject out of hand her harboring of "parasites and exploiters" in her novels, but he aims at the same time to keep free of the timidly relativistic historicists, who defend her narrow social views by pleading the limited perspective of her period.[10] We should the more easily accept Kettle's differentiations of valid and invalid social criticism had he been equally discriminating in his account of the class society Jane Austen describes. He refers to "the values recommended by *Emma*" as "the assumptions of aristocratic society," whereas later he accepts the Marxist description of the author as "a genteel bourgeoise 'reflecting' the views of her day." He does, indeed, go on to declare the author to be broader than "a conventional member of her class, blindly accepting its position and ideology," but by this time we may well wonder which class is meant.

Upon reflection, we can see that the terminology of class structure in descriptions of Jane Austen is used — even by critics intent upon refining the grosser forms of Marxist criticism — mainly for political color, not for sociological description based on historical evidence of stratification. "Bourgeois" and "aristocratic" in the above-quoted phrases mean little more than rich (how rich?), con-

servative (Tory? Old Whig?), and snobbish (toward which classes?). In contrast to the imprecision of her commentators, Jane Austen herself is quite precise about how much money her characters
have, the source of their income, and their attitudes toward members of other classes. If Jane Austen was a defender of the upper
classes, it behooves her critics to know the criteria of her class distinctions, the social tensions between the classes of her time, and
the degree to which the author both reflects her own class's view
and diverges from it.

We should remind ourselves, as Mrs. Leavis has urged, that Jane
Austen spent the first twenty-four years of her life in the eighteenth
century and was a devotee of Dr. Johnson. The usual approach to
the eighteenth-century aspect of her work is the antiquarian one of
her editor, R. W. Chapman, symbolized by the reproductions in his
edition of period costumes and other chic paraphernalia. The tendency of the Janeites to cherish the antique for its own sake need
not detract from the serious social investigation of her work. It is
time for both historical approaches to pool their resources. A mine
of unanalyzed ore is stored up in crotchety letters to the *Times
Literary Supplement*, Chapman's copious notes, and other antiquarian data that have accumulated through the years.

When this material is critically employed, Jane Austen's writings
will be seen to appear at a crucial point in the transition of English
society to the modern age: at the point when the fear that the
French Revolution would spread to England caused a cultural reaction which gave its peculiarly conservative cast to much of English Romanticism.

Romanticism has been given more definitions even than those
collected by Lovejoy, but an essential element of the English Romantic movement is the almost uniform turning of the first generation of poets to conservative, traditionalist, and nationalist values.
Perhaps the most cogent explanation of this shift has been offered
by the historian Crane Brinton, whose "anatomy" of the course
of reaction deserves to stand with his "anatomy" of revolution.

Brinton's thesis implies that it was not only the Jacobin scare that
caused Wordsworth, Coleridge, and Southey to renounce their

libertarian ideals. An equally strong fear of the rising middle class and of laissez-faire economic competition led them to seek the sanction of their ideals in the memory of an organic community whose values could be resurrected for future reform movements. Brinton continues:

. . . they sought for objects to which men could become attached, objects stable in themselves but capable of slow growth through the devoted efforts of men. This attachment must be mystic; that is, men by a mystic surrender of their freedom to the service of the loved object must feel that this surrender has really added to their freedom by adding to their importance. The nation, the Church of England, the romantic traditions of the Middle Ages, the family, all seemed to these poets objects worthy of loyalty; and around them they cast an atmosphere of what in Germany is called "Gemütlichkeit," and in England "middle-class morality." [11]

Without claiming that Jane Austen stands in the same organicist tradition with these philosophical poets, it is important to see that the values they found in nation, family, tradition, religion — the values, in part, of *Mansfield Park* — are not opposed to the Romantic revolt but are its historic outgrowth and fulfillment. Jane Austen no more ceased to be a Romantic when she wrote *Mansfield Park* than Wordsworth did when he wrote *The Prelude*; in these works their early exuberance is transformed into a stabler and more profound vision, reaffirming new values by the authority of the old.

From this standpoint, we are able to clarify the frequent view that *Mansfield Park* is a reversion to the taste and style of the Augustan Age — that it censures the libertine morality of the Romantic movement. Whereas her earlier works, *Northanger Abbey* and *Sense and Sensibility*, criticize the excesses of Romantic emotion, *Mansfield Park* marks no retreat from the synthesis of Romantic verve and Augustan restraint which Jane Austen achieved in *Pride and Prejudice*. Trilling in particular has contrasted the latter two novels, and has found the value of Elizabeth Bennet to be rejected in the characterization of Mary Crawford, with a new type of virtuous heroine recommended in the person of Fanny Price. But if we read *Mansfield Park* as life-denying — *Pride and Prejudice-*

denying — we shall have trouble understanding why, in the same letter in which she announces that her new novel will have a "complete change of subject — ordination," Jane Austen says of Elizabeth Bennet, "I must confess that I think her as delightful a creature as ever appeared in print, and how I shall be able to tolerate those who do not like *her* at least I do not know." [12] The balance of values in both *Pride and Prejudice* and *Mansfield Park* becomes more susceptible to calibration when these novels are set in their time, for Romanticism itself is a balance of conservative and libertarian values.

In determining the extent to which *Mansfield Park* is a critique of Romantic values or an affirmation of the late Augustan society it portrays, we shall come to rephrase many of the questions that are habitually asked of the novel. Instead of employing the fact that Jane Austen came under Evangelical influence during the years 1811–13 simply to explain a presumed moralizing tone in the novel, we shall explore how this influence shows itself in the treatment of that "complete change of subject — ordination" and its reflection of the religious life of society. In the same vein, rather than assume that the rejection of the amateur theatricals is grounded in their moral impropriety (which no character but Fanny declares), we shall ask why Jane Austen chose a politically and socially tendentious play for her characters to reject. Avoiding the usual display of bad temper which describes Fanny Price as a prig, we shall examine those of her values which are characteristically Romantic, to determine the degree to which they act as a criticism of Mansfield Park itself. Finally, to make more precise the usual description of the novel as a defense of the aristocratic way of life, we shall consider the effect on the gentry of the political and economic transformations of the time, to see how the novel assesses that class's strengths and weaknesses in facing the challenges of its moment in history.

In this way, we may come to see the measure in which the artist merely reflects her times and the measure in which she transcends them. Once immersed in the complexities of the historical situation, we discover that a major writer can no more offer blanket affirmations of a society's or a class's way of life than she can wholly reject it. Jane Austen's social criticism and social values are much more specific than most of her modern readers are aware. Her Evangelicalism expresses itself not in moralizing but by suggesting the need for clerical reform. Her apparent prudishness regarding the play is an implicit critique of an oversophisticated aristocracy and its dalliance with radical intellectual currents. Her creation of a singularly unattractive heroine allows her to oppose the Romantic virtues of the heart to the predominantly mercenary motives of the gentry. From this complex set of judgments, it will be seen that the novel does not take sides with the gentry, but instead takes that class's historical situation as its *donnée* — and then seeks out a way to survive within it.

III

The Novel in Its Time

THE reading of *Mansfield Park* has from the first had to contend with Jane Austen's announcement, in a letter to her sister, that its subject was to be ordination. The obvious deficiencies of the statement as an account of the novel's action have led to a number of critical embarrassments and justifications. Perhaps the only consistent impression that has emerged is that the concern for Edmund's ordination suits the moralizing tone of the novel and of its author at that point in her career. To deal with this and other critical cruxes, the reader can profit from a greater-than-ordinary number of facts about the historical setting of the novel. Jane Austen, as a daughter of the country clergy, takes her subject from the concerns of that class and of its patrons, the gentry.

A datum of bald historical evidence has recently been provided by Clarence L. Branton in a note on Jane Austen's treatment of ordination.[1] Branton is content to establish two small points: that Jane Austen's clergymen are ordained priests without first becoming deacons, and that the ordinations in her novels occur at uncanonical times. Assuming that a clergyman's daughter who was also a scrupulously accurate writer would have informed herself on such matters, the readiest conclusion is that these events in the novel mirror conditions of the time. By having her clerical figures perform so naturally what the Evangelical reformers would have looked on as abuses, she is subtly highlighting the shortcomings of the gentry-dominated social order and its religious institutions. But she is not, as Mrs. Leavis and other critics have suggested, passively echoing the Evangelical sentiment of the day.[2]

Similar criticism of the clergy occurs in other novels (we have only to recall Mr. Collins of *Pride and Prejudice*), but it is given special force by the ironic situation in *Mansfield Park*. After a sustained defense of his choice of the clerical vocation against Mary Crawford's well-founded remarks about its contemporary undignified worldliness, Edmund Bertram, the nominal hero of the novel, finds righteous union with Fanny Price. He is ultimately established as rector of Mansfield, becoming, as it were, its spiritual arm, and affirming symbolically the alliance of the gentry and the Established Church.[3] Yet this almost lyrical conclusion of the novel rests on the shaky foundation of an improperly executed preparation for the priesthood and induction into it.

There is an even more serious offense to religious scruples to offset the novel's apparent vindication of the Church. One of the burning issues for the Evangelical movement was the ineffectuality of a church organization that by condoning multiple incumbency failed to insure the performance of the pastoral functions of a living religion. The clerical equivalent of absentee ownership, "pluralities" (as they were called) are the target of vigorous censure by the proprietor of Mansfield, Sir Thomas Bertram himself, speaking of Edmund:

"His going [to the rectorship of Thornton Lacey], though only eight miles, will be an unwelcome contraction of our family circle; but I should have been deeply mortified, if any son of mine could reconcile himself to doing less. . . . a parish has wants and claims which can be known only by a clergyman constantly resident, and which no proxy can be capable of satisfying to the same extent. Edmund might, in the common phrase, do the duty of Thornton, that is, he might read prayers and preach, without giving up Mansfield Park; he might ride over, every Sunday, to a house nominally inhabited, and go through divine service; he might be the clergyman of Thornton Lacey every seventh day, for three or four hours, if that would content him. But it will not. He knows that human nature needs more lessons than a weekly sermon can convey, and that if he does not live among his parishioners and prove himself by constant attention their well-wisher and friend, he does very little either for their good or his own." (Ch. XXV, pp. 247–248.)

Yet the same gentleman later effects the acquisition by his son of these two livings eight miles from each other. When they are first married, Fanny and Edmund are content with the living at Thornton Lacey, but "just after they had been married long enough to begin to want an increase of income," the living at Mansfield becomes available. They readily take it up, at the expense of the spiritual welfare of the parishioners (as indeed — in the absence of a textual statement to the contrary — it may be understood that Thornton Lacey is retained).

In the background of all discussions of the clerical profession at the time was a public issue that makes the action in the novel even more distinctive. The first parliamentary campaign of the Evangelicals was designed to mitigate the abuses of multiple incumbency, at least in its impact on the curates, the underpaid clergy who did the work of the parish in the absence of the titular office-holders.[4] In the years 1812–13, a cabinet under the Evangelically influenced prime minister Perceval was able to put through a bill establishing a graded series of minimum salaries for curates, proportionate to the size of their parishes. During the very years in which the novel was written, then, the issue of multiple incumbency was a *cause célèbre* of English national life.

Setting the novel against this background can render intelligible the otherwise disproportionate amount of detail devoted to the clerical profession. Mary and Edmund are not directly debating the "concept of duty," as Lionel Trilling would have it. They are discussing the then-lively issue of the relative poverty of clergymen who lack multiple incumbencies. Edmund's principles lead him to defend his choice of career while acknowledging the meanness of the way of life of those without substantial livings (he does not yet know that he will have two). He bases his defense on the virtue of the work, but he is forced to admit Mary's charge that his choice is favorably influenced by the guarantee of a good living in his father's patronage. Edmund's subsequently renouncing Mary to follow his vocation is not, however, allowed to become a tragic choice, for as soon as he marries Fanny he acquires his second parish, thus allowing him to measure up, if not to his Evangelical ideals, at least to the living standards of his class.[5]

The only condition that might explain the imperfections of Edmund's ordination and of his subsequent clerical career is the failure of his and his father's practice to reflect their righteous, perhaps Evangelically inspired, principles. Jane Austen's primary interest seems, then, to be not in the purification of the Church — the Evangelicals' prime target — but rather in the moral criticism of the gentry. Her object is self-evaluation in the gentry, not its conversion. To this end, she is willing to employ Evangelical criticisms not only against the clergy of the Church of England but also against the religious values of the gentry. After the appearance in 1797 of Wilberforce's *A Practical View of the Prevailing Religious System of Professed Christians in the Higher and Middle Classes in This Country Contrasted with Real Christianity*, the practical paganism not only of the libertine aristocracy but also of the solid gentry became a favorite target of the Evangelicals. Since *Mansfield Park* is designed to criticize the weaknesses of the gentry, it takes up the barrenness of that class's "High-and-Dry" religious practice.

The religious condition of the gentry is dramatized when the Mansfield party takes the equivalent of a "stately-homes" tour of Sotherton, the estate of Mr. Rushworth, the ill-fated fiancé of Maria Bertram. The current spiritual state of the Rushworths — and, by extension, of their class — is revealed when the party comes to the domestic chapel, "fitted up as you see it, in James the Second's time." Mrs. Rushworth expatiates on its genteel antiquity, revealing in passing an utter disregard for its religious meaning:

". . . It is a handsome chapel, and was formerly in constant use both morning and evening. Prayers were always read in it by the domestic chaplain, within the memory of many. But the late Mr. Rushworth left it off."

"Every generation has its improvements," said Miss Crawford, with a smile, to Edmund. (Ch. IX, p. 86.)

In such passages, Jane Austen parallels the Evangelicals' effort to save England's ruling class from the erosion of its religious bulwarks and the politically dangerous growth of the skeptical doctrines of the Enlightenment.[6] They did so primarily by calls for religious conversion, but there is no suggestion that Jane Austen shared the intensity of their religious faith. Her values are better represented in Fanny's feelings about the chapel, which emphasize the secular rather than the religious values that have been lost. She enlarges the discussion of the chapel's former use and present abandonment by expressing the value of historical tradition as such: " 'It is a pity . . . that the custom should have been discontinued. It was a valuable part of former times. There is something in a chapel and chaplain so much in character with a great house, with one's ideas of what such a household should be! A whole family assembling regularly for the purpose of prayer, is fine!' " It should be clear that her values are only tangentially religious: domestic worship is to be revived not to save souls, but to fulfill a social ideal — "what such a household should be!" This ideal is not merely that of the family but of the historical community: the organic ties of national life that give England its stability and strength, and which must be reasserted to repel attacks from without. These are the organicist values of Burke and the Lake poets, and in Fanny's expression of them Jane Austen echoes their conservative Romanticism.

In keeping with the contemporary tendency to stress the value of organic social ties and religious revival for secular purposes, not only Sotherton but Mansfield itself is shown to fall far short of the ideal. The two country houses are not distinguished by their religious practices, though their inhabitants are in varying degree religiously principled. Mansfield, too, has no domestic chaplain, no regular weekday worship; its people show no marked religious fervor. Edmund, like all Jane Austen's clergymen, is strikingly devoid of religious doctrine or sentiment. But his dedication to the clerical calling is a step toward religious vitality. Religious affirmation there is in the novel, but — as it was in the Evangelical criticism of the time — it is put to the service of maintaining the strength of the gentry, bolstering its self-assurance and correcting its lapses, in the face of the threats of a revolutionary age. Like their author, her characters are to govern their lives "without presuming to look forward to a juster appointment hereafter" (Ch. XLVIII, p. 468).

A knowledge of the political implications of events in *Mansfield Park* will afford us a clearer view of the amateur theatricals than the long-sustained commentary on them has thus far been able to provide. Historical evidence about the theater and audience of the time has not been lacking, but the critics have focused on *Lovers' Vows*, and have failed to develop the play's relation to the non-theatrical preoccupations of the age.

The first historical study of the theatricals, published by William Reitzel in 1933, provided a thorough summary of contemporary responses to the theater, ranging from the Evangelicals' attack on all "mummery" to the specific immorality of many contemporary plays.[7] Reitzel's evidence is marshaled to convince us that by the standards of the time *Lovers' Vows* was an "improper" play, to be condemned by Fanny, Edmund, and Sir Thomas on moral grounds. Subsequent critics have made much the same assumption while changing the grounds of moral judgment. Trilling supposes that the rejection of theatricals stems from a Platonic tradition which distrusts acting because it fosters the vices of the characters by imitation; other writers have vaguely ascribed the traditional hostility to "Puritans."

Evangelical, Platonic, and "Puritan" attitudes were, no doubt, at work at the time,[8] but it is remarkable that none of these attitudes can be pointed out in the novel during the debate about the performance. It is easy to disprove the influence in the novel of any such blanket condemnation of theatrical performances by remarking Tom Bertram's statement in defense of the project: he reminds the doubters that Sir Thomas had himself supervised recitations from plays during their childhood (Ch. XIII, pp. 126–127). Edmund, arguing against the performance, claims that this childish reciting was for the sole purpose of improving their elocution. Yet if Sir Thomas were Puritan, Platonic, or Evangelical in his attitudes toward the stage, his children's moral corruption would have been a high price to pay for their training in declamation.

And corrupted they would have been, according to the traditional theories, for one of the stock speeches Tom remembers having recited in his youth is from *Douglas*, by John Home. By the beginning of the nineteenth century, *Douglas* had become a respected repertory piece, but it had been banned by the Presbytery when first performed at Edinburgh, on the grounds of its moral defects.[9] There were, from an orthodox standpoint, good arguments for the moral disapprobation of *Douglas*. The plot includes the heroine's marrying against her father's wishes (breaking her oath); attempted seduction (by the villain, to be sure); a trap to catch a supposed adulteress in the act (actually it is mother and son who embrace); a duel to the death between a son and his stepfather; and finally, the suicide of the mother. These sordid events are described or enacted in the refined language of moral idealism, and Sir Thomas was probably no more to be shocked by *Douglas* than he would have been by *Lovers' Vows*, which is also written in the clichés of eighteenth-century sentimental drama. Yet there is a difference in social reputability between these plays, even though there is little difference in the propriety of the subject matter. For all its melodramatic grotesquerie, its primitivistic rudeness and Gothic extravagance (which Thackeray mercilessly satirized in *The Virginians*), *Douglas* lacks the peculiar qualities which make *Lovers' Vows* unacceptable at Mansfield Park.

In determining the grounds of its unacceptability, we must discriminate the special motives of the characters in the opposition camp. Edmund is troubled by a sense of the impropriety of any large-scale diversion in the absence of his father, who is making a hazardous voyage in wartime. Fanny is most troubled by the specific roles assigned to the residents of Mansfield: the pairing of the engaged Maria and her admirer Crawford seems to her — and indeed becomes — an opportunity for flirtation (curiously, their roles are those of mother and son), while the pairing of Mary Crawford with Edmund arouses her jealousy and its accompanying moral indignation. Sir Thomas's principal motive seems to be his own comfort: he rejects the performance, not the play. Yet we can detect in his expressions of personal convenience an implicit judgment on the play — or at least on the social milieu with which it is historically associated.

The play is proposed for performance at Mansfield by Mr. Yates, a visitor (who subsequently elopes with Julia Bertram). If anything can be said to act as an immediate cause of Sir Thomas's closing of the theaters, it is the naive and vulgar enthusiasm with which Yates pursues his play madness. When Yates leaves the house, Sir Thomas is glad to be rid of "the worst object connected with the scheme" (Ch. XX, p. 194). We have here more than personal distaste. Even though Sir Thomas does not make his prejudices explicit to the modern reader, a contemporary would have had little difficulty in sensing the class antipathy in his judgment of the performance as a whole, and of Yates in particular.

Yates has brought the stage fever with him from another country house, Ecclesford, where the performance of *Lovers' Vows* had been regretfully canceled because of a death in the family. In the aristocratic set at Ecclesford, the proprietor, Lord Ravenshaw, a duke, and at least one other nobleman had been cast as the villainous aristocrats. When Sir Thomas rejects the theatricals and the play itself, he renders a judgment of the taste and pursuits prevalent among the aristocracy of the time.[10]

To savor the full significance of this social antagonism in the upper classes, we must be aware of the political implications of such plays in the period of the Napoleonic wars. *Lovers' Vows* is one of a large number of German plays that were translated and revised for English taste at this time. German influence on the English stage reached its peak at the turn of the century. Wordsworth in his preface to the second edition of *Lyrical Ballads* takes it as a symptom in his critique of contemporary society as "acting with combined force to blunt the discriminating powers of the mind."

The Novel in Its Time

Among other forces of disintegration like the French Revolution, the Napoleonic wars, and the shift of population to the cities, he includes the theatrical tastes of the upper classes: "To this tendency of life and manners the literature and theatrical exhibitions of the country have conformed themselves. The invaluable works of our elder writers . . . are driven into neglect by frantic novels, sickly and stupid German Tragedies, and deluges of idle and extravagant stories in verse." [11]

Strange to say, August Kotzebue, the author of this play, was more popular in England than either Goethe or Schiller.[12] To seek the reason for this anomaly brings us to the special character of *Lovers' Vows*: it is Continental political radicalism expressed in the conventions of sentimental comedy. It was not shocking to an English audience to find the villains aristocrats, but it was dangerous to hear the aristocracy as a class denounced as villainous. Mrs. Inchbald's efforts to curb her radical spirit in "translating" Kotzebue's plays for an English audience merely resulted in a substitution of local radical sentiments for Continental ones; e.g., in Act II, scene 2, of *Lovers' Vows* (reprinted in the Chapman edition of *Mansfield Park*, p. 498):

Count. Who is Mr. Anhalt?
Amelia. Oh, a very good man. (*With warmth.*)
Count. "A good man." In Italy, that means a religious man; in France, it means a cheerful man; in Spain, it means a wise man; and in England, it means a rich man. — Which good man of all these is Mr. Anhalt?
Amelia. A good man in every country, except England.

Lovers' Vows, for all its banality, is by virtue of its glancing blows at social values — the unpunished profligacy of the aristocrats and their hypocritical anathemas against those they seduce — an effective condemnation of the ruling classes.

The play's detractors in the *Anti-Jacobin Review* and *Gentleman's Magazine* were quick to see the political danger of harboring such sentiments in a nation at war with republicanism, and William Cobbett (in his newpsaper, *The Porcupine and Anti-Gallican Monitor*) summed up the attack: "Lovers' Vows, the natural son of Kotzebue, is not among the least objectionable dramas of German notoriety. It is the universal aim of German authors of the present day to exhibit the brightest examples of virtue among the lower classes of society; while the higher orders, by their folly and profligacy, are held up to contempt and detestation." [13]

The attack on Elizabeth Inchbald, the adapter of *Lovers' Vows*, was even more specific in its political bias than that on the play. *The True Briton*, for example, found in her works the seeds of revolution and censured them in much the same terms Burke used to attack English adherents of the French Revolution. Indeed, Mrs. Inchbald was intimately connected with Thomas Holcroft, Robert Bage, Charlotte Smith, and other writers who carried the ideals of the Revolution into English literature. Like them, she was the author of sentimental novels — the most successful *Nature and Art* — arguing the natural goodness of man, which can emerge only when he is freed from the corrupt and despotic institutions of monarchies and aristocracies. The same sentiments emerge in *Lovers' Vows* when it portrays in an attractive light the frank wooing of a man by the sincere young heroine, Amelia. They are present when it fulminates against the decadent aristocracy represented by Count Cassel, who tries to force her to marry him without love, and by Baron Wildenhaim, who has debauched the simple heart of Agatha, the illegitimate mother. It is not only the age's sense of sexual propriety that was shocked by such displays of feeling, but its social and political attitudes as well.

On the other hand, those who favored the libertarian German dramas did so on political grounds — even, in the case of Hazlitt, against their own better moral and aesthetic judgment:

The action is not grave, but extravagant: the fable is not probable, but improbable: the favourite characters are not only low, but vicious: the sentiments are such as do not become the person into whose mouth they are put, nor that of any other person: . . . the moral is immorality. In spite of all this, a German tragedy is a good thing. It is a fine hallucination: it is a noble madness. . . . It embodies . . . the extreme opinions which are floating in our time; . . . we are all partisans of a political system, and devotees to some theory of moral sentiments. [14]

Starting from the opposite political position, the detractors of the play went on to condemn its moral and aesthetic failings. That their fears of the dangers of radical dramas were justified is suggested by the immediate consequence of rehearsing *Lovers' Vows* at Mansfield: the scene painter brought in for the occasion quickly makes "five of the under-servants idle and dissatisfied" (Ch. XX, pp. 190–191).

Sir Thomas's rejection of the theatricals is, however, only indirectly a defense against their revolutionary potential. His immediate enemy is the aristocracy, in the person of Mr. Yates. Sir Thomas does not reject *Lovers' Vows* itself, but he resents the frivolous diversions of his family which he finds upon his return from a perilous wartime transatlantic voyage. Whereas the main antagonism of Fanny and Edmund to the play is the casting of partners for the purposes of flirting, Sir Thomas does not share this personal motive. He stops the rehearsals before he learns details of either the play or the cast, basing his decision on the transformation of his house into an aristocratic theater (and, incidentally, on being himself comparatively neglected in the fervor of the theatrical fad). His wish to preserve the decorum of Mansfield Park is, at bottom, a wish to prevent its becoming an Ecclesford, the seat of an effete class and its self-destructive tastes. Laying aside Jane Austen's subtlety in referring to topical affairs, we may say that in the rejection of the theatricals the Tory gentry criticizes the Whig aristocracy's flirtation with the culture of the French Revolution.

The heroine of *Mansfield Park*, a teen-age poor relation who had been raised in an inferior position among the children of the house, has been almost universally derided for her priggishness. In spite of Fanny's moralizing language, which smacks of an earlier age, and despite the apparently Romantic features of her rival, Mary Crawford, it is Fanny who emerges as a Romantic heroine. When the denouement makes Fanny victor over Mary, it does not work the triumph of gentility and traditionalism but proposes a Romantic, corrective view of the gentry as a class.

In an obvious way — so obvious, perhaps, as to prevent earlier critics from explicitly noting it — Fanny is the kindred spirit of Marianne Dashwood and other Austen heroines of sensibility. Witness her response to a moonlit landscape:

"Here's harmony!" said she, "Here's repose! Here's what may leave all painting and all music behind, and what poetry only can attempt to describe. Here's what may tranquillize every care, and lift the heart to rapture! When I look out on such a night as this, I feel as if there could be neither wickedness nor sorrow in the world; and there certainly would be less of both if the sublimity of Nature were more attended to, and people were carried more out of themselves by contemplating such a scene." (Ch. XI, p. 113.)

Thus, in the language of the eighteenth-century Sublime, is expressed a Romantic view of nature's moral influence.[15] Fanny is the only one in her set to be much affected by the beauty of landscape. Fanny's "Enthusiasm," as Edmund calls it, is not a desirable trait in the eyes of the Bertrams and their class; the word enthusiasm connotes, during this period, the irrational and unrespectable religious ardor of the lower-class Wesleyan converts, who embodied a revolt against Augustan decorum which ran parallel with Romanticism.

In her Romantic response to landscape, Fanny is directly contrasted with Mary Crawford. It is odd that Mary has acquired the reputation of being the Romantic in the novel, for Jane Austen labors to ascribe to her a Johnsonian preference for the city to the country — not merely a taste for urban high society but a conscious choice of civilization over nature. She characteristically applies to herself an aphorism of the court of Louis XIV: "I see no wonder in this shrubbery equal to seeing myself in it." To Fanny's rhapsodies over landscape, "untouched and inattentive [Mary] had nothing to say." The authorial voice concludes the contrast in summary fashion: "She had none of Fanny's delicacy of taste, of mind, of feeling; she saw nature, inanimate nature, with little observation; her attention was all for men and women, her talents for the light and lively" (Ch. VIII, p. 81). Mary, far from being the Romantic heroine manquée, is portrayed — through her connection with vice in high places (her uncle, the Admiral), with a worldly set of cheating wives (Mrs. Fraser and Lady Stornaway), and with an ethos of refined nihilism — as the exemplar of aristocratic decadence. Her closest literary relations are with the witty, vamp-like heroines of Restoration comedy.

Though Henry owns an estate in Norfolk and plays at being a squire and an "improver," the Crawfords represent the metropolis in the country environment of Mansfield. The urbane style of these urban visitors is made clear in differences of ethical and religious values. The distinction between the moralities of city and country underlies the perennial debate between Mary and Edmund about his vocation. She charges:

"*You* assign greater consequence to the clergyman than one has been used to hear given, or than I can quite comprehend. One does not see much of this influence and importance in society, and how can it be acquired where they are so seldom seen themselves? How can two sermons a week . . . govern the conduct and fashion the manners of a large congregation for the rest of the week? One scarcely sees a clergyman out of his pulpit."

"*You* are speaking of London, *I* am speaking of the nation at large."

"The metropolis, I imagine, is a pretty fair sample of the rest."

"Not, I should hope, of the proportion of virtue to vice throughout the kingdom. We do not look in great cities for our best morality. . . ." (Ch. IX, pp. 92–93.)

Nor is this difference confined to religious issues: the city — as the custodian of Neoclassic humanism, opposed to the country realm of Romantic nature — represents an aesthetic norm which is criticized in the action of the novel. The cultural implications of Fanny's Romantic taste emerge in her response not to nature but to the past. It has been observed that Fanny quotes Cowper against "improvers" of the landscape — "Ye fallen avenues, once more I mourn your fate unmerited" — and the conclusion has been drawn (e.g., by Charles Murrah[16]) that she is simply effusive over the Picturesque, in the eighteenth-century manner. A closer examination of her response to improvements reveals that she regrets not the loss of the trees of a relatively wild, natural landscape (it is, after all, *regular* avenues that she regrets in the quotation from Cowper), but rather the loss of the traditional associations of the trees, their connection with a long family history. By the same token, Fanny judges the Renaissance architecture of Sotherton — and the lapsed religious life of the family — not on aesthetic or religious grounds but on the grounds of their lack of Gothic antiquity: "This is not my idea of a chapel. There is nothing awful here, nothing melancholy, nothing grand. Here are no aisles, no arches, no inscriptions, no banners. No banners, cousin, to be 'blown by the night wind of Heaven.' No signs that a 'Scottish monarch sleeps below.'" (Ch. IX, pp. 85–86.) Even if the ideas were not specific enough, the allusions to *The Lay of the Last Minstrel* would link Fanny's attitudes to Scott. This is the conservative Romantic attitude toward landscape, architecture, and history: things acquire value not merely by being old but by being connected with the organic life of the nation.

The link with Scott's conservatism emphasizes the novel's close relation to the political debates of the day. Burke's affirmation of the national spirit as it is manifested in its institutions and traditions was designed to rally the upper classes to the struggle against France and against revolutionary tendencies at home. Thus Fanny in expressing her own taste echoes a politically charged doctrine. But the classes to which such affirmations of tradition are addressed do not — either in the novel or in contemporary history — respond: not only is Mr. Rushworth planning to bring in the well-known landscape architect Humphrey Repton for extensive improvements, but Mansfield Park itself is "modern, airy and well situated" — values indeed, but not the values of a gentry conscious of its roots in the past. The discussions of landscape "improvement" in the novel therefore sound a note prophetic of the gentry's political weakening and decline.

Though the political overtones of Fanny's tastes do not directly challenge the gentry at Mansfield Park, her related attitudes toward love and marriage come into open conflict with the gentry's social and economic interests. Her attitudes are not, it must be acknowledged, uniquely — although they are typically — Romantic, nor is the marriage market into which she is placed confined to the gentry. Yet the dramatic working of *Mansfield Park* places Fanny in the role of a critic of her society, and makes the novel's emphasis again fall on the correction of the gentry's way of life.

The issue comes to a crisis when Fanny, who has long cherished the unresponsive Edmund and has formed a moral antipathy toward Henry Crawford, is pressed by Sir Thomas to marry the latter. Because her scruples prevent her revealing why she disapproves of Crawford, her refusal is without an apparent motive, but it is patently sincere. Sir Thomas's answer embodies perfectly the system he is part of:

"I had thought you peculiarly free from wilfulness of temper, self-conceit, and every tendency to that independence of spirit, which prevails so much in modern days, even in young women, and which in young women is offensive and disgusting beyond all common offence. But you have now shewn me that you can be wilful and perverse, that you can and will decide for yourself, without any consideration or deference. . . . The advantage or disadvantage of your family — of your parents — your brothers and sisters — never seems to have had a moment's share in your thoughts on this occasion. . . ." (Ch. XXXII, p. 318.)

Sir Thomas's attack is charged with the mercenary and authoritarian attitudes that Jane Austen customarily treats with contempt and which, in almost all her works, are a major stumbling block between the heroine and happiness.[17] Fanny, on the other hand, is placed in the role of simple virtue assaulted by upper-class worldliness — a common enough theme in earlier fiction and one especially popular in pre-Romantic and Romantic tales like that of Fanny Price's namesake, a heroine in Crabbe's *The Parish Register*.[18] The authorial voice sums up the issue between Fanny and Sir Thomas at the close of their argument: "Romantic delicacy was certainly not to be expected from him" (Ch. XXXIII, p. 331). Romanticism is here a critical, though not a revolutionary, force which refines and humanizes accepted values.

Sir Thomas, by preferring worldly advancement over honest love (and, although unknown to him, over good morals as well), shows the habits of mind of the corrupt aristocracy. His arguments are identical with those of the London world, expressed when

Mary pleads her brother's suit to Fanny. The upper classes — the gentry and the aristocracy — are equally indifferent to the virtuous heart. But Fanny, surprisingly, should rank with such Romantic heroines as the revolutionary libertine of *Lovers' Vows*. It has been claimed by some critics of the theatricals that *Mansfield Park* is constructed in direct opposition to the play, so that its moralistic heroine is the obverse of the self-assertive and amoral Amelia. It may now be seen, however, that Fanny and Amelia are alike, not opposite, in their preference for a poor country curate to a brilliant match — in their "wilful and perverse" choice of honest poverty over worldly fortune.

Mansfield Park has been generally assumed to be a defense, even a celebration, of the gentry's way of life, but after examining Fanny's opposition to that way of life we can no longer believe that Mansfield represents the good society. Sir Thomas's bullying of Fanny is not an isolated instance of the failure of the country-house ideal; his own marriage to a woman of utter immaturity results in failures of education which lead their children to broaden the circle of dissolution. The system that matches the inane Rushworth and the spoiled Maria Bertram leads straight to the "guilt and misery" of her deserting him for Henry Crawford. The failure of the gentry to educate its young results also in the elopement of the younger daughter, Julia, with the corrupt aristocrat, Mr. Yates. Fanny's resisting Sir Thomas's marriage arrangements becomes, in the event, a means of establishing the marriage market as one of the gentry's institutions most in need of reform.

The Romantic ideal is defended in *Mansfield Park* not only by Fanny Price but, curiously enough, also by Edmund. In the endless debates about marriage and a clerical career in which Edmund and Mary Crawford engage, he upholds his commitment to his station and its duties against her ideal of a rich and worldly life. Here love and wealth, not duty, are opposed, and Edmund manages to maintain his passion for Mary and his religious calling with equal force. The result of this debate — in which the usual roles of the sexes are amusingly reversed, the demure young man holding out against the woman's urbane seductions — is to pair Edmund, the follower of his virtuous heart, with Fanny, and to distinguish them from almost everyone else about them. These two are the flower of life at Mansfield Park, and though it is a pale flower, it is hardy enough to survive at the close of the novel, when the children of Mansfield who have lived by the values of their class wither into bitter fruit.

Once the contemporary sources and references of *Mansfield Park* are recognized, it is no longer possible to regard the novel simply as a defense of the society it portrays — any more than it is simply an attack on it. The Evangelical influence in the novel's moral tone serves, dramatically, to expose the failings of religious life among the gentry, with even the nominal heroes of the novel guilty of the fashionable abuses. The affair of the theatricals implies not the exclusion of modern culture from the good society but the weakness of the aristocracy in its indulgence of political enemies at a critical historical moment. The heroine of the novel becomes, by her commitment to Romantic ideals of nature, tradition, and love, the deviant from and ultimately the apostle to Mansfield. But the survival of Mansfield and of the gentry as a class is called into doubt by yet another matter of concern in the novel.

The gentry at the time the novel was written was, despite its deep roots and current prosperity, open to a potential source of economic crisis, and its condition demanded serious re-examination by those worried about its future. Landholders had entered a period of prosperity about 1785, rents increased as much as five-fold between 1790 and 1812, and the 1773 and 1781 Corn Laws (looking forward to the 1815 "Famine Law") put a premium on domestic agriculture; all this made the time the heyday of the landed classes. "Never was country-house life more thriving or jovial," writes G. M. Trevelyan. Unfortunately, he goes on to remark: "In the mirror that Miss Austen held up to nature in the drawing-room, it is hard to detect any trace of concern or trouble arising from the war." Yet even in economic matters, we see that her mirror *does* reflect the concern and trouble, perhaps more than the thriving joviality.

The year 1812 was marked by the Luddite riots, the assassination of the prime minister (the above-mentioned Spencer Perceval), the war with the United States, the trial of the Hunts (following shortly upon the release of Cobbett from two years' imprisonment), and the agitation of Sir Francis Burdett and other independent Whigs in Parliament (Byron delivered his maiden speech against the Frame Work Bill). Rumors of revolution were rife, and England resembled an armed camp not only along the Channel but in the counties stirred by industrial unrest. Though this profound agitation is not reflected directly in the Austen novels, the economic peril of the gentry is an underlying tension in *Mansfield Park*.

In 1812, even before the close of the Napoleonic wars and at the time the novel was being written, agricultural prices began to fall; by 1816 the condition approximated economic depression. *Mansfield Park* is set, then, at a turning point in the gentry's fortunes. Almost at the beginning of the novel, the Bertram estate, though it appears prosperous, is revealed to be encumbered by perceptible limitations; Mrs. Norris blurts out that the family's "means will be rather straitened, if the Antigua estate is to make such poor returns" (Ch. III, p. 30). The inference is that the Mansfield holdings are insufficient to maintain the style of life which the novel describes. This estate — which presumably represents an entire socioeconomic class — is not self-sustaining but depends for its existence on colonial landholdings. We are to see Sir Thomas as a "West Indian," with the contemporary connotations both of admiration and of contempt for the nouveau riche.

In the midst of the action, Sir Thomas is called upon to visit his estate in Antigua. Critics have tacitly assumed that he is removed from the scene merely to allow the theatricals episode to develop and to provide the climactic return in which he cuts them off. But what are we to make of the fact that Mansfield is not a self-sufficient estate, that the family's way of life is threatened, and that the large and airy rooms depend on an external and troubled colonial holding for their support? And if a question about offstage action may be admitted, what does Sir Thomas *do* in Antigua to make secure the sources of his income?

Here again, the modern reader must be aware of public knowledge so widespread at the time that it need not be set out in the novel to have its effect in explaining the action. Some facts of economic history may explain the bearing of these questions on the novel's theme and provide a broader view of the class it is concerned with. At the time in which the novel is set,[19] the domestic agricultural crisis was matched by a depression in the British West Indies.[20] As early as 1805, the islands' local governments had declared themselves bankrupt, and by 1807 many plantations had failed. The difficulties were rendered almost paralyzing by Napoleon's Continental System, which closed most European markets to West Indian agricultural exports (mainly sugar). Sir Thomas could have done little to relieve the pressure of international politics on his plantation, but he might have sought to diversify the prevailing one-crop agriculture, which had caused an economic problem in the first place by exhausting the soil, and then made the depression worse for the islands because they were totally dependent on the largely European sugar trade, now lost. This possibility is lent credence by the fact that, as an absentee landlord, Sir Thomas would have been an exception on Antigua, which had prospered more than the neighboring islands, where absentee ownership was the rule. A vigorous estate owner would have had to be physically present to make the large-scale planting decisions required at precisely that critical time.

Another task Sir Thomas is likely to have been engaged in was related to a problem with far more profound effects on the colonial economy. The year 1807 was the year of the Act for the Abolition of the Slave Trade, and nowhere could the act have been felt more heavily than in the British West Indies. It is wrong to suppose that these long-established slave colonies had no need for the further importation of slaves (the act forbade only slave shipments, not slavery itself); the record tells us that conditions of life and work were so bad that the slaves failed to reproduce and survive in sufficient numbers to provide an adequate, stable labor force. The deficit was made up by continued imports of slaves, but with abolition the future of the colonies looked bleak. The prime requisite was to improve the condition of the slaves; humanitarianism took root among the colonists on these sound economic grounds. The job Sir Thomas is likely to have been seeing to, then, was the elementary one of assuring that his slaves did not die so readily of underfeeding, overwork, and the overseers' brutality. If the passage refers to his own experience rather than to politics in general, it might be his contact with slavery that causes Tom Bertram, after his return from Antigua, to remark to the clergyman, Dr. Grant: "A strange business this in America, Dr. Grant! — What is your opinion? — I always come to you to know what I am to think of public matters." (Ch. XII, p. 119.)

Public matters do not, to be sure, enter the dialogue except as passing allusions, but their moral influence is felt in the context of Evangelicalism. If there is an Evangelical strain in *Mansfield Park*, we should expect to find in it some indication of Jane Austen's awareness of the Evangelicals' campaign against slavery. We know from her letters that she had read a work by Thomas Clarkson, the author of *The Abolition of the African Slave Trade*, and one of the few writers on public affairs she mentions. Though the novel does not develop Sir Thomas's experience in Antigua, a personal consequence of his voyage suggests that it was a profound one. After his return, he shows a marked change of temperament, pre-eminently in his relations with Fanny but also in his awareness of the failings in his establishment — particularly the baleful influence of Mrs. Norris (Ch. XLIII, p. 465: "His opinion of her had been sinking from the day of his return from Antigua"). Though he had formerly joined her in abasing Fanny because of her class origins, now he treats Fanny as a favorite child. How are we to account for this changed moral sensibility, which eventually issues in the discovery of his "executive weakness" [21] in the education of his children?

Offstage action becomes even more difficult to speculate upon when it concerns the development of character, and we shall be no more secure in our reading of Sir Thomas's inner workings than we are in our reading of Hamlet's. Since the novel, like the play, may be accused of lacking an "objective correlative" of the protagonist's emotion, it is possible to reconstruct his experience only

hypothetically. He goes to Antigua as a planter, presumably opposed to abolition; he occupies himself, for economic reasons, with
improving the slaves' condition; he acquires some of the humani-
tarian or religious message of the Evangelical and other mission-
aries laboring in the same vineyard; and he returns critical of his
own moral realm, with a warmer feeling for his young dependent, a
sterner rejection of aristocratic entertainment (especially that with
a marked revolutionary content), and a strong defense of his son's
dedication to resident pastoral duty.

But the Bertrams are dead to moral experience; it is Fanny alone
who is concerned about Sir Thomas's experience of slavery, as she
tells Edmund:

"Did not you hear me ask him about the slave trade last night?"
"I did — and was in hopes the question would be followed up by
others. It would have pleased your uncle to be inquired of farther."
"And I longed to do it — but there was such a dead silence! And
while my cousins were sitting by without speaking a word, or
seeming at all interested in the subject, I did not like . . ." (Ch.
XXI, p. 198.)

In any account of the reasons for Sir Thomas's sudden preference
of Fanny over his own children, her absorption in his Antigua and
other experiences must rank high: she is ready to identify herself
with the fortunes of the family and the issues confronting its class,
while his own children are not.

If some such process is at work, we may see, in Sir Thomas's development, the leaders of the gentry forming more humane social
attitudes — although too late to enforce them thoroughly in conduct (he acts like an ogre toward Fanny when it is a question of a
financially sound marriage, even after his personal affection for her
has begun to emerge). This renewal of moral concern about social
life reflects the worldly motives of Evangelicalism, which proposed a religious revival for the gentry in an attempt to shore up
that class's antiquated ideological position, to strengthen it in its
political struggle against radicalism. *Mansfield Park* may be read as
a dramatic record of the gentry's effort to work out a more vigorous ideology, to correct its internal failings, and to modify its tra-

ditional way of life in response to changed political and economic circumstances.

Jane Austen writes little about the aristocracy and almost nothing about the bourgeoisie in their struggle for supremacy in the age of the industrial and French revolutions. Yet she holds a unique place in the history of the social novel by speaking to and for the gentry as it was affected by those revolutions. Her novels do not take a position with respect to any political ideology; she is trying to discover subtle readjustments in the daily life of her own class. D. W. Harding has well described Jane Austen's relation to her society: "Her object is not missionary; it is the more desperate one of merely finding some mode of existence for her critical attitudes." [22] When we realize that these attitudes are not confined to personal relations but extend to all aspects of social life, then the historical understanding of Jane Austen's subject matter will have enriched our critical response to her art.

APPENDIX TO CHAPTER III

The structure of the landed classes at the beginning of Jane Austen's time has been well formulated by G. E. Mingay in *English Landed Society in the Eighteenth Century* (London and Toronto, 1963). Mingay carefully distinguishes "great landlords" and "gentry" on the criterion of an income of £5,000 a year, the minimum required to maintain not only a country house but also a town house — "The great house and the London season were the essential status symbols of the great landlords" (p. 19). Only some four hundred families could qualify for the higher class, and despite an economic fluidity which enabled some baronets and even commoners to enter it, this was an aristocracy composed mainly of noblemen. The gentry, on the other hand, ranged from a level which Mingay describes as "wealthy" down through "squires" to "gentlemen." The criteria by which they are distinguished are the £3,000 and £1,000 a year marks respectively. (In addition, Mingay describes a class of "freeholders" of the "better" and "lesser" sorts with incomes ranging from £700 to £30 a year; see the table on p. 26 of his work.)

The Novel in Its Time

The exact designation of the Bertrams' class in *Mansfield Park* is, for all Jane Austen's well-known explicitness in matters of money, somewhat vague. Mr. Rushworth, with his annual £12,000, is clearly among the great landlords; Henry Crawford, with his £4,000, ranks among the wealthy gentry (his income apparently comes from Everingham, his estate in Norfolk, although he disdains to live there). But Sir Thomas's income is never told, though we know that his wife's £7,000 was said to be a poor dowry, considering his own wealth. By the time of the action, however, the family has given up its town house and Sir Thomas is forced by Tom's debts to sell the living at Mansfield to Dr. Grant, instead of keeping it for Edmund as he had planned (Ch. II, p. 20; Ch. III, p. 23). In addition, the threat posed by the Antigua difficulties — whatever their origin — suggests that the family's domestic income was limited. The estate at Mansfield suggests solid property holdings and a want of ready money: it includes "a park, a real park five miles round, a spacious modern-built house, so well placed and well screened as to deserve to be in any collection of engravings of gentlemen's seats in the kingdom, and wanting only to be completely new furnished" (Ch. V, p. 48). The Bertrams are probably, we must conclude, of the wealthy gentry, if not of the squires.

It might nevertheless be asked whether the considerable opulence of Mansfield and Sir Thomas's baronetage entitle the family to be called aristocratic. The term is and has been vague and honorific, and in present-day usage it is often applied to the gentry. *The New English Dictionary* lists both broad and narrow nineteenth-century uses of "aristocracy," but a constant criterion is the possession of *privileges by birth*. As the historian Henry Hallam put it in 1838: "The distinguishing characteristic of an aristocracy is the enjoyment of privileges which are not communicable to other citizens simply by anything they can themselves do to obtain them." By such a criterion, the rank of baronet is inherently ambiguous: it is the only hereditary order which gives rank, precedence and title *without privilege*. Standing as he does between the peerage and the knightage, it is understandable that Sir Thomas's status has been open to vague interpretations.

There exists, however, a suggestive indicator of contemporary feeling about the status of baronets: their position in *Burke's Peerage* or other social registers. The introduction to the 1963 edition recalls the arrangement of *Burke's Peerage, Baronetage and Knightage* at its inception in 1826: "John Burke and his successors have from quite early days, though not from the very start of Burke's Peerage, dealt with Baronets on the same footing as Peers." The first quarter of the nineteenth century was a time of social retrenchment, in which rigid distinctions gave way to a merging of baronets with the nobility. But if, as Burke's procedure suggests, this gradual process was not yet complete in 1826, baronets like Sir Thomas must at the time of the novel's action still have been placed a cut below the nobility. If true conservatives like Burke are the arbiters appropriate to Sir Thomas, the Bertrams are not of the highest, the aristocratic class.

IV

The Psychology of Moral Character

SOONER or later he who seeks to defend Fanny Price against the dyspeptic rage of her critics tends to claim for her a higher moral level than the other characters in the novel. Her attackers have shown themselves committed to a morality of vitality and freedom — which Lionel Trilling, referring to the Crawfords, has called "secularized spirituality" — so that a defense of Fanny becomes the assertion of a competing moral standard, one of religion, duty, and restraint. Such controversy substitutes ethical for literary standards of judgment, yet it is probably impossible to talk of character without touching moral issues. How can critical inquiry be made in such a way as to convert ethical judgments into aesthetic ones? It should be possible to talk of Fanny's character and even of her moral being without erecting an absolute ethical system in which to measure her. We can, moreover, read in Fanny's experience an intimate record of the operation of a moral disposition within a total personality. Far from presenting Fanny as a sanctified moral being, Jane Austen presents her as a complex tangle of impulse and restraint: hers is a test case for the psychologist of morality.[1]

It is again Mary Lascelles who best corrects our angle of vision on Fanny, by considering the evidences of Jane Austen's own attitude toward her:

For her other heroines she means us to feel as we feel for friends and lovers; but for Fanny as for a creature less well furnished for offence and defence than those with whom she is compelled to live. Among the Bertrams she is like a mortal among giants. That is why, contrary to her author's general rule, we are allowed first to make her acquaintance when she is a child; why we are more than once reminded of her childhood afterwards. . . . It is tenderness as towards a child that is implied in Jane Austen's use of a phrase exceptional with her — "my Fanny." [2]

We can, then, begin to see Fanny not as a paragon of virtue who, despite her author's intention, offends us, but rather as an object of sympathy. She is a frail spirit fighting the battle of life with weapons inadequate to cope with the society in which she exists. We can see the moral judgments she makes not as providing the ethical doctrine of the novel but as making up one strand in the web of morality and psychology that is the substance of Jane Austen's human world.

The weaving of this web goes on throughout Fanny's anguished life at Mansfield, but its main features emerge most clearly in her relations with her parents. When she is greeted with indifference on her arrival at her Portsmouth home, her response is given in painful detail:

She was at home. But alas! it was not such a home, she had not such a welcome, as — she checked herself; she was unreasonable. What right had she to be of importance to her family? She could have none, so long lost sight of! William's concerns must be dearest — they always had been — and he had every right. Yet to have so little said or asked about herself — to have scarcely an enquiry made after Mansfield! It did pain her to have Mansfield forgotten; the friends who had done so much — the dear, dear friends! But here, one subject swallowed up all the rest. Perhaps it must be so. The destination of the Thrush must be now pre-eminently interesting. A day or two might shew the difference. *She* only was to blame. Yet she thought it would not have been so at Mansfield. No, in her uncle's house there would have been a consideration of times and seasons,

The Psychology of Moral Character

a regulation of subject, a propriety, an attention towards every body which there was not here. (Ch. XXXVIII, pp. 382–383.)

This passage typifies Fanny's mind, with its mixture of self-abnegation and hostility, of egoistic claims and frosty judgments of others, of snobbish embarrassment for her parents, even of jealousy of her favorite brother. Her affirmation of Mansfield can be read as grudging approval of her rich relations based on the hope — not yet the achievement — of greater personal recognition there. It is this kind of evidence that is overlooked by the critics who have hated Fanny's so-called priggishness, thinking they have caught faults in her character which the author either did not perceive or did not consider faults. It is from such backhanded justifications of Mansfield that they have concluded — without reference to who makes these judgments and the situations in which they are made — that the novel is a defense of aristocratic manners.

Fanny is presented not as a paragon of virtue but as a weak woman with self-defensive and self-aggrandizing impulses who, because of her economic dependency and her social inferiority, is forced to adopt what Alfred Adler has called a feminine, submissive style of life. (A fuller statement of his theory will be given in the following chapter.) The offensive weapons of submissiveness are her society's store of conventional moral attitudes. It is these that make Fanny the sanctimonious critic of everyone — literally everyone — in her world but her brother William (with the inconsistency noted above). As a compensation for the psychic costs of submissiveness, Fanny's hostility expresses itself in moral aggressiveness. Though she cannot give vent to her judgments in public, she makes up amply in private, talking to herself and to those (usually Edmund) who can accept her morality as in accord with her submissiveness.

One critic, Lord David Cecil, keenly perceived this interaction between Fanny's professions of selflessness and all-too-human selfishness,[3] but he was unwilling to grant that the interaction was intentionally designed by the author and consequently dismissed it as beyond the range of her knowledge. That such mechanisms were not beyond the psychological intuition of the time is shown by the similarity of Fanny's defense mechanism to Mrs. Norris's method of aggression through assumed martyrdom. The creator of Mrs. Norris was patently conscious of her characters' masks of self. The psychology of Jane Austen's novels is clarified by modern discoveries, but it is not dependent on them.

Fanny exhibits not only the origins of moral aggression in psychic needs but also the possibilities of moral awareness through heightened introspection. Fanny is often in an emotional chaos that isolates her in the midst of her society: she can, for example, tell no one of her love for Edmund. She is the only character in the novel who is amply conscious of her relations with others, but by that very awareness she is isolated. Mansfield is a world that makes genuine personal connection all but impossible while it makes each of its members altogether dependent on social ties.

Fanny's discomfort within the prison of her consciousness, and her dissatisfaction with her submissive-aggressive style of life, rise to a crisis under the onslaught of Henry Crawford's charm. We begin to be drawn to her as we watch her feeble attempts to apply a moral judgment to him which will protect her emotions from his. Her morality continually proves inadequate to the complexities of mature experience and must therefore continually be bolstered with fresh supplies of hostility, greater indignation. We can feel only sympathy for Fanny's incapacities in her personal relations, for her inability to understand the reality of sexual passions such as Edmund's for Mary and Henry's for herself. Perhaps most poignant of all her limitations is her inability to accept the love Mary offers her, because it does not fit into the moral order she is committed to maintain.

I do not mean to imply that Fanny's morality is to be rejected as disguised egoism, but suggest rather that it is to be neither affirmed nor rejected but understood. The novel is designed to study the intimate — though not necessarily causal — relation of her morality to her total personality. In the view of the writers who have seen this novel as simply a set of moral dicta, she is not a subject of study but a moral spokesman; in the view set forth here, she is the main human *subject* of the novel. And what we study more closely than anything else in her is the course of her feelings and their expression in subjective perceptions and judgments.

Since Fanny is the main character of *Mansfield Park*, she is also a means of our coming to know and evaluate the other characters. In part this happens because she is the "reflector" or narrative point of view from which the story is told. But since Fanny's marked subjectivity renders her a classic example of what Wayne Booth has described as the "unreliable narrator," [4] it is not her moral judgments but the structure of her character that gives her a focal position in the novel. Fanny is the measure — certainly not the ideal — of human existence in *Mansfield Park*. With the ample means we are given to help us understand her psychology and its expression in morality, we can turn to each of the other important characters and analyze the corresponding relation between his emotional drives and the style of life he creates for himself. It becomes possible at the same time to learn more of Fanny by measuring her against the other characters in the novel. We have here one of the first instances of the nineteenth-century concern for the nature of selfhood, defined here by the precarious forms in which the characters submerge, disguise, or express their deepest impulses.

The first variation on the theme of selfhood is exhibited by Lady Bertram, who builds a life style on a related form of self-suppression. Instead of repressing her desires she asserts them, to the exclusion of every other consideration. But she is like Fanny in assuming a passive role: not that of a moral superior but that of a moral neuter — not by renouncing her pleasures but by extinguishing all strong feelings. She stands in a group of Austen figures — Mr. Woodhouse, the father of Emma, is the nearest approximation — who are so devoted to personal comfort, static ease, and emotional noninvolvement as to exemplify better than any other literary characters the Freudian theory of the death wish, the tendency to return to inorganic existence. Thus Professor Trilling has suggested that Lady Bertram is an appealing figure whose total self-absorption makes her, ironically, attractive to us; presumably it is our own death wish to which the appeal is made.

A Reading of *Mansfield Park*

What is the function of the comic irony with which Lady Bertram is presented? Part of the irony — which becomes near-tragic — is that for all her blissful ignorance she is unable to remain unconscious of the demands of others' needs and feelings: she cannot succeed in shutting out the world. Further, in relying utterly on the authority of Sir Thomas, Lady Bertram is shown to be avoiding the demands not only of reality but also of morality. Throughout the novel the author never finds herself too busy to say a few words on Lady Bertram's inadequacy to the moral situations in which she is called upon to act. Edmund cannot induce her to prohibit the theatricals; she will not condone giving Fanny a horse without Sir Thomas's approval, but she allows her daughter to become engaged, "with all due reference to the absent Sir Thomas"; "to the education of her daughters, Lady Bertram paid not the smallest attention"; "to know Fanny to be sought in marriage by a man of fortune, raised her, therefore, very much in her opinion" — even though Fanny has counted on her aunt to prevent her marriage to a man she does not love; and so on. To some readers her naivety is virtuous, but the action of the novel shows it to be a fugitive and cloistered virtue, which the world this side Eden will not allow to live in peace.

While Fanny's life style of censoriousness is shown to be insufficient for the complexities of life, Lady Bertram's corresponding use of benign indifference to protect her own satisfactions is more dramatically proved inadequate. Jane Austen's courage in shaking this comic creation — whom, no doubt, she loved — out of the peace of blissful ignorance is one of the great aesthetic achievements of *Mansfield Park.* When Lady Bertram writes Fanny about Tom's illness, even Fanny is willing to detect the insincerity we all perceive; but when Lady Bertram sees her son on the verge of death, she is shocked out of her torpor and for the first time becomes a moral being. She does so by virtue of *feeling* itself — by that sensibility which it has been her constant effort to avoid.

If Lady Bertram's role in the novel is to illustrate a type complementary to Fanny's — in which feeling is repressed for the sake of moral disengagement — another character exhibits the danger of creating one's identity not by repression but by feeling itself. Henry Crawford is all sensibility, free of inhibition, but spontaneity must, we learn, be tempered and refined — without drying up its sources. He is a natural actor, the best of the amateur company, one able to project himself into any type of character. He is a Romantic actor, like Kean as contemporaries describe him. In Keats's terms, he has "negative capability," in Hazlitt's, "sympathetic imagination": the artist's lack of egoism that allows him to be possessed by the objects he experiences, even to the loss of his own identity. Although desirable for the artist, such lack of determinate selfhood is dangerous to the moral personality — he "was every thing to every body" (Ch. XXXI, p. 306), the classical Sophist ideal. His nature is attractively affectionate, and warms even Fanny, "because he really seemed to feel" (Ch. XXXVI, p. 365). And his love for Fanny, in turn, leads him to profit from the influence of her better balance of reason and emotion: "he had rationally, as well as passionately loved" her (Ch. XLVIII, p. 469). But he loses himself in a blaze of feeling — "he had put himself in the power of feelings on [Maria's] side, more strong than he had supposed" (Ch. XLVIII, p. 468) — and runs off with her in a wildly self-destructive climax.

For all the dangerous volatility of Henry's feelings, feeling itself is not denied in *Mansfield Park*. It is Fanny's objection to Henry's flirting during the theatricals that he has behaved "improperly and unfeelingly" — and "improperly" is further defined as hurting Mr. Rushworth's feelings (Ch. XXXV, p. 349). Feeling can, as in all Jane Austen's novels from *Sense and Sensibility* to *Persuasion*, both ruin and redeem, and the Crawfords are almost redeemed by their love for Fanny and Edmund. It is feeling that betrays them, most bitterly in Henry, who will go on to be punished by his sense of loss, of having thrown away his chance at happiness with Fanny when within sight of winning her. Nothing in the novel, finally, serves to negate the judgment of Mary which the author passes in her own voice — when she speaks of the "really good feelings by which she was almost purely governed" (Ch. XV, p. 147) — nor the judgment of Henry which Edmund expresses in almost the same terms: "those feelings have generally been good" (Ch. XXXV, p. 351).

Between the extremes of selfhood by extinction of feeling and selfhood entirely created by feeling, Fanny stands as a slightly tarnished golden mean. In her style of life, morals and perceptions are strongly influenced but not limited by feeling. Her negative reaction to Portsmouth is a case in point: in spite of her moral disposition to honor her parents, she is hurt when her need for recognition and affection is denied, generating a string of carping criticisms of her home[5] (Henry visits and finds it easy to overlook its faults — probably not from mere politeness). But Fanny is surprised to find that she is able to love her father after all. In conversation with Henry — while Fanny is blushing with shame for her father's anticipated boorishness — the latter shows himself a man among men, ready to take up such masculine subjects as ships and trade. Feeling emerges at last, and Fanny begins to mature at once in her morality and in her emotions. We do not see her full development in the novel; indeed, in some of our last views of her (quoted in the last chapter of this study) she is as adept as ever at inventing moralistic expressions of personal hostility. Yet her patient conquest of Edmund and her marriage to him are the fulfillment of as constant an emotion as is recorded in the world of Mansfield Park; what it lacks in vibration it makes up in a quality which is, Jane Austen says, beyond her power to describe: "Let no one presume to give the feelings of a young woman on receiving the assurance of that affection of which she has scarcely allowed herself to entertain a hope" (Ch. XLVIII, p. 471).

The permutations of the term "feeling" evolve, as we trace them, into a structure of meaning: the values and dangers of feeling make up one of the novel's central themes. This evolving definition of meanings is a touchstone of what might be called the "grand style" in English fiction. Jane Austen's style has never been paid the kind of attention her more flamboyant or expressive successors receive; Howard Babb's *Jane Austen's Novels: The Fabric of Dialogue* [6] closely follows the nuances of implication in interpersonal relations, but a sustained study of her diction, metaphor, and imagery remains to be written. In *Mansfield Park*, such a study would proceed from certain words whose repetition establishes them as thematic keys, much in the manner of Shakespeare's iterative images. Most often these words appear first in simple contexts and acquire wide resonance as they reappear in crucial situations. Such are the words "evil" and "connection" (both used upwards of twenty-five times), first confined to their conventional references — to anything troublesome and to marriage ties, respectively — and later expanded to suggest opposite poles in an ethic of human commitment. A few samples from each process may suffice:

Such and such-like were the reasonings of Sir Thomas — happy to escape the embarrassing evils of a rupture (Ch. XXI, p. 201); . . . Fanny was worn down at last to think every thing an evil belonging to the ball (Ch. XXVII, p. 267); "The evil lies yet deeper" (Edmund on Mary Crawford; Ch. XLVII, p. 456); [Sir Thomas] clearly saw that he had but increased the evil, by teaching [his children] to repress their spirits in his presence (Ch. XLVIII, p. 463); He had felt her as an hourly evil (Sir Thomas on Mrs. Norris; Ch. XLVIII, p. 465); To be relieved from her, therefore, was so great a felicity, . . . there might have been danger of his learning almost to approve the evil which produced such a good (Ch. XLVII, p. 466).

. . . a Lieutenant of Marines, without education, fortune, or connections (Mr. Price; Ch. I, p. 3); [Sir Thomas's] desire of seeing all that were connected with him in situations of respectability (Ch. I, p. 4); . . . Mrs. Price could no longer afford . . . to lose one connection that might possibly assist her (Ch. I, p. 4); [Julia and Fanny] were two solitary sufferers, or connected only by Fanny's consciousness (Ch. XVII, p. 163); "I feel that we are born to be connected" (Mary to Fanny; Ch. XXXVI, p. 359); "Connected, as we already are, and, I hope, are to be, to give up Mary Crawford, would be to give up the society of some of those most dear to me" (Edmund to Fanny; Ch. XLIV, p. 422); "The families would never be connected, if you did not connect them" (Fanny's reply; Ch. XLIV, p. 424).

Another effect produced by Jane Austen's verbal technique is the crescendo of meaning in individual chapters when a word sounds repeatedly with constantly augmented force. One such crescendo appears in Chapter XXXVI, when the use, eight times in ten pages, of the word "heart" by and about Mary Crawford marks a turning point in our belief in the sincerity of her sensibility. The famous sentence — "Let other pens dwell on guilt and misery" — which begins the final chapter is only the midpoint of another such crescendo:

The horror of a mind like Fanny's, as it received the conviction of such guilt, and began to take in some part of the misery that must ensue, can hardly be described (Ch. XLVI, p. 440); . . . it was too horrible a confusion of guilt . . . the simple, indubitable family-misery (Ch. XLVI, p. 441); . . . if it were indeed a matter of certified guilt and public exposure (Ch. XLVI, p. 442); . . . so many were miserable (Ch. XLVI, p. 443); . . . guilt and infamy (Ch. XLVII, p. 449); Let other pens dwell on guilt and misery (Ch. XLVIII, p. 461); What can exceed the misery of such a mind [Maria's] in such a situation? (Ch. XLVIII, p. 464); [Rushworth's] punishment followed his conduct, as did a deeper punishment, the deeper guilt of his wife (Ch. XLVIII, p. 464); Maria's guilt had induced Julia's folly (Ch. XLVIII, p. 467).

Since most of the above uses occur in association with the word "evil" in these final chapters, the last movement attains the intricacy of counterpoint.

Any linguistic summary of these passages would shatter the fragile web of implication they generate. Yet it may not be a gross oversimplification to derive from them a moral norm: whatever destroys human connections is an evil. There is no preordained code in Jane Austen's ethical workings; value is assigned empirically on the basis of observable consequences for personal and social fulfillment. The Crawfords' feeling seeks to link others to themselves, but the instability of the links thus formed leads to painful severances. Fanny's priggishness cuts her off from others and hides their value from her, but her commitment to her beloved is strong and lasting. She exerts the power of feeling at its best, and subtly employs her moral itch in the service of her passion, when she skillfully lands Edmund by sympathizing with his broken heart. We remember, to her credit, that much — even sanctimoniousness — may be justified in the cause of love.

The Psychology of Moral Character

The main form of connection is imaginative sympathy. For the most part, Fanny's consciousness extends to but does not embrace the persons in her environment, but occasionally she breaks through her self-imposed bonds. This union of selves is represented symbolically near the midpoint of the novel, as Fanny prepares herself for her first ball. She has been given a gold cross by her brother, a fancy necklace by Mary, and a plain gold chain by Edmund — with a moral consistency almost allegorical. Delighted that the cross neither literally nor figuratively fits the necklace, she is free to combine the gifts of Edmund and William, those most dear to her. But in a burst of generosity rare in the world of Mansfield Park she decides to wear the necklace too: "She acknowledged it to be right. Miss Crawford had a claim . . ." (Ch. XXVII, p. 271).

It remains for us to consider the significance of the marriage of Fanny and Edmund, which stands as the highest achievement in the culture of Mansfield. We are asked to celebrate it with all its limitations and to see its shortcomings as resulting from the limitations of that society. To evaluate Fanny's and Edmund's marriage we must consider their potential but unfulfilled marriages to the Crawfords.

Edmund's rejection of Mary is not, strictly speaking, moral, for Mary *does* nothing immoral — though she nervously talks like a libertine to minimize her brother's guilt. The inner workings of Edmund's mind remain obscure to the end, but it should be clear that throughout his romance the confrontation with a woman as highly developed as Mary, sexually and socially, is an uncomfortable challenge for him. When his reluctant courtship is finally blighted, Edmund joins Fanny in excoriating Mary's moral levity, seizing the opportunity to relieve his wounded feelings. Morality is again put at the service of feeling and changes from a defensive to an offensive weapon. But clearly Edmund does not much enjoy his righteous indignation as a substitute for sexual fulfillment: his is a gloomy redemption.

The lesson of feeling and morality learned by readers of the novel, though not by the hero and heroine, is that a life lived by repeatedly using morality for defense and attack is likely to be a self-limiting life. Like Edmund's resistance to Mary, Fanny's rejection of Henry is not born of moral conviction, for Henry has up to that point *done* nothing beyond flirting with Maria during the rehearsals. Nor is it born of antipathy, for Henry rapidly succeeds in making himself attractive: he has the graces of a gentleman and the attentiveness of a sincere lover. Her negative views of Henry are called forth to meet a situation to which she cannot adequately respond: her dominant mood is confusion at the evident passion of Henry's proposal and at the sudden necessity for her to take passion seriously. The appropriate reaction to such confusion is regression; once Fanny cannot subsume an event under the categories of her morality, she acts (and admits that she writes) like a child (Ch. XXXI, p. 308). In this way she avoids the challenge to become a woman that Henry has laid down.

Fanny and Edmund are, then, as limited by their moral rigidity as the Crawfords are limited by their sensibility. Mary and Henry, after their blasted childhood, are prepared to deal with the world by means of their social and sexual charm, but Henry's erotic feeling proves too weak to sustain him in his pursuit of Fanny. Mary's charm, too, is not great enough to overcome external circumstance when the tragedy of the other Bertram children leads Edmund away from her. Their story develops, then, not the evil of passion but its relative weakness among the media of personal connection.

Their failure does not, however, justify an absolute rejection of the Crawfords' life style because it is based on feeling; it serves to point out the dangers encountered by those who live so. Henry's experience offers the same lesson as Mary's. In one of the most remarkable revelations of her moral vision Jane Austen concludes:

Could he have been satisfied with the conquest of one amiable woman's affections, could he have found sufficient exultation in overcoming the reluctance, in working himself into the esteem and tenderness of Fanny Price, there would have been every probability of success and felicity for him. His affection had already done something. Her influence over him had already given him some influence over her. Would he have deserved more, there can be no doubt that more would have been obtained. . . . Would he have persevered, and uprightly, Fanny must have been his reward — and a reward very voluntarily bestowed — within a reasonable period from Edmund's marrying Mary. (Ch. XLVIII, p. 467.)

Jane Austen's severe tone toward the Crawfords, as in this passage, is not merely an echo of Edmund's and Fanny's judgment of them but expresses her bitter acknowledgment of reality — of human indifference to the power of love to transcend personal isolation. Fanny sees Henry's and Mary's conduct only as the inevitable outcome of their character, but Jane Austen sees her characters as free, and this makes her hate them momentarily when they willfully neglect their possibilities of self-realization. It has been well said that ". . . as it reads at present, we are bidden contemplate, not the triumph of evil, but certainly what is not far removed from it, the failure of goodness: Edmund and Fanny could *not* redeem the Crawfords; not by example, nor by the influence of love." [7] Wherever we place the source of the failure, it is clear that the greater hope, the marriage of opposites who could spiritually complement each other, has been lost.

The union of Fanny and Edmund is not meant to represent the ideal, just as that of Fanny and Henry or of Edmund and Mary would not have represented it. The resolution of the novel is fitting, considering the persons involved, but the ideal lies in the marriage of another set of characters, like these but more responsive to the possibilities within themselves of synthesis. As in *Pride and Prejudice*, where despite the vigorous personalities of hero and heroine, their capacity to change becomes the source of their harmony, an ideal marriage in *Mansfield Park* would have been the completion of Fanny's and Edmund's potentialities rather than what it is, a confirmation of them in their characters. Their marriage is rather like that in *Sense and Sensibility*, where we are not meant to think of Marianne Dashwood's marriage to the dull Colonel Brandon as representing the highest type of life possible, but only as the outcome of many errors in judgment, an outcome showing the final inadequacy of the assumptions and tastes on which those judgments were based. By the same token, we are not asked to regard Fanny and Edmund as the ideal couple but only as the possessors of rewards appropriate to their merits — each other.

Even with this muted resolution, the novel suggests the possibility of closer connection in the future, of an improvement in the next generation of family life at Mansfield Park. For the union of Fanny and Edmund, no matter what its shortcomings, is superior to the marriage with which the narrative opens: the marriage of Sir Thomas to Lady Bertram, based primarily on the attraction of her empty beauty, which led to all the failures of education that the novel traces in the lives of their children. In the course of the action, the Bertrams as a family are improved by pruning and grafting: Maria, Julia, and Mrs. Norris are ejected from Mansfield and Fanny and Susan are welcomed into it. What the family seems to need is a tougher, less attractive couple to guide its fortunes, and at this low point in its history Fanny and Edmund are admirably suited to take command.

V

The Structure of the Myth

CRITICS with a penchant for psychological speculation are often surprised to discover their acutest perceptions unconsciously suggested by their anti-Freudian competitors. It is as though the theory of repression were applicable to scholarship as well as to other kinds of behavior: the hostile critic fails to see the unwelcome realities. A case in point is an exceptionally thorough study of *Mansfield Park*, which, though it focuses on the social and educational implications of the novel, three times suggests that its structure is that of a fairy tale, yet avoids giving this suggestion sustained consideration.[1] It has been widely assumed that this and other Austen novels are laden with themes of childhood fantasy — the repressive or irritating parents, the misery of growing up, the final winning of a beau — but most critics have failed to bring these suggestions to bear on the novels' total form.

The time is past, however, for anxiety that great works of art will be sullied by revealing their burden of universal human fantasies and mythic plot forms. Even if one does not follow Dr. Jones to the last thread in his unspinning of the web of *Hamlet*, it is by now acknowledged that that play can be dramatically and ethically illuminated by adducing its primitive psychic content. In literary character analysis, as in the preceding chapter, few will now insist on excluding all psychological evidence and terminology. When we see Fanny making up for her childhood's weaknesses in an alien environment by developing a repertoire of submissive traits and hostile moral attitudes, there seems little difficulty in using the term "feminine" in its Adlerian sense to describe the life-style of passivity. We may venture, then, a short step further and perhaps win another terminological insight from Adler's description of this personality type:

. . . Such traits as timidity, indecision, insecurity, shyness, cowardliness, increased need for support, submissive obedience [which Adler later calls "dishonest obedience"], as well as phantasies and even wishes, which one can summarize as ideas of "smallness" or masochistic tendencies, correspond to the inferiority feeling. Above this network of personality traits there appear, with defensive and compensatory intent, impudence, courage, impertinence, inclination towards rebellion, stubbornness, and defiance, accompanied by phantasies and wishes of the role of a hero, warrior, robber, in short, ideas of grandeur and sadistic impulses.

The inferiority feeling finally culminates in a never-ceasing, always exaggerated feeling of being slighted, so that the Cinderella fantasy becomes complete with its longing expectation of redemption and triumph.[2]

So plausible — indeed so self-evident — does this characterization seem that we are tempted further into the tale of Cinderella for its potential archetypal bearing on the novel.

Cinderella is not only a frequently met character type in reality but also a universal figure in folklore. Her elementary situation is the pattern for innumerable stories in literary history and proto-history.[3] These tales are usually rife with magic transformations into and back from animals, and replete with grotesque murders — often cannibalistic. Yet besides its closeness to the infantile strata of the mind, the myth refers to a more public and conscious realm: the denial of and struggle for property, which reflects ancient practices of inheritance.[4]

Like the curious preference for the younger son so often found in the book of Genesis, the Cinderella myth is a reflection of societies in which, not without challenge, the younger child customarily inherited the economically crucial property. Since such an arrangement must often have excited sibling rivalry and blood feuds, these tales may be legends based on real events. The moral that they impress is, therefore, the younger son's or daughter's successful defense of his property rights through heroic and disciplined action.

To see *Mansfield Park* in this company of tales is to gain access to one of its central concerns, the selection of Fanny Price as the fit inheritor of a dominant position in the house, in preference to the corrupt daughters of the proprietor. Fanny is ten years old when she arrives at Mansfield; she is the eldest daughter of her parents but the youngest of the children among whom she is to be reared. (She is only eighteen, on the threshold of maturity, when the major action of the novel takes place.) It is, of course, not simply her position as the youngest that makes Fanny a Cinderella, but also her position as a poor dependent, the psychic equivalent of an orphan. When Mrs. Norris puts into effect her intention that Fanny should be "the lowest and the last," she puts on the traditional accoutrements of the wicked stepmother — down to the strong odor of a witch. Fanny is not, to be sure, made a scullery maid, but her cousins, like stepsisters, domineer over her while the parental figures remain unaware of her misery. Then, after showing her moral worth in the theatricals, Fanny is given the chance to go to the ball. But Henry Crawford, her Prince Charming, is, ironically, offensive because of his very attractiveness — reversing the usual adolescent wish-fulfillment. Fanny wants, it appears, not the prince but the surrogate fairy godfather, Sir Thomas, or his younger reflection in Edmund.

Since Fanny is selected for triumph not because of her physical but because of her moral qualities, she becomes the subject of a test not of the size of her foot but of her loyalty to her potential inheritance, i.e., a test of her alienation from her parents. When she commits herself to Mansfield — overlooking its abasement of her — by despising her Portsmouth home, when she is fully committed to her new father and father figure, if not to her substitute mother and sisters, she is given the opportunity to triumph over her rivals, and they are brought low by their own wickedness. While her cousins are humiliated and the harridan Mrs. Norris is excluded from the house, she marries into personal domination, if not financial possession, of her adoptive home, and displaces her cousins in the heart of her true father, Sir Thomas. The structure of the fairy tale is an object lesson in character formation: Fanny overcomes her childhood weakness by developing moral implements for self-preservation, and when presented with the weakness of her tormentors she employs these tools with sufficient strength to prevail over them. The storybook lesson is not stinted: the final page speaks of "the advantages of early hardship and discipline, and the consciousness of being born to struggle and endure."

If this were the extent of *Mansfield Park*'s relation to the Cinderella story it would remain simply a parallel, showing the universality of girlish daydreams but not elucidating the special form of the novel. To find that form, it is necessary to examine not only the congruence of the novel's plot and the fairy tale's but also the structure of the former in its own right. The usual sequence of events in an Austen novel is a series of arrivals at and departures from the seat of the action (following closely the normal course of life for a sedentary country family). The twist given to this normal plan in *Mansfield Park* is that arrivals and departures here signify a struggle for effective — moral or psychological, if not material — control of the estate itself. The chief influence of the Cinderella story lies in the vital matter of inheriting property. Fanny is at first the child without a dowry, with no expectations, who must be reared without raising her hopes of wealth — as Mrs. Norris and Sir Thomas agree at the outset. Eventually she inherits not the estate itself but a commanding position in the affections of the family. This broad development from exclusion to possession, together with the fluctuations of arrival and departure that mark the gaining and losing of footholds, is the structure of *Mansfield Park*.[5]

The major events in the novel may be schematically represented, taking the course of existence at Mansfield Park as a baseline and

The Structure of the Myth

indicating arrivals and departures by directional lines, as shown in the accompanying drawing. From this paradigm it can be seen that the first movement of the novel is one of entries: the assembling of forces and the display of their characteristics on the visit to Sotherton. The middle movement is centered on the theatricals: it is, in effect, a struggle to change the moral tone or spiritual possession of Mansfield. The theatricals are made possible by the removal of Sir Thomas, initiated by the parallel entry of Mr. Yates, interrupted by the proprietor's return, and ended with the removal of the in-

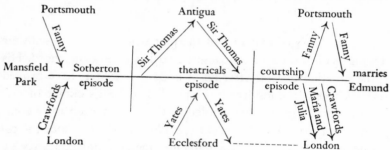

terloper. The final movement traces the temporary withdrawal of Fanny and her triumphant return. Her victory comes about through the disintegration of the family in her absence, and through the removal of all who stand opposed to her. The minor patterns formed by these movements, too, are noteworthy: Fanny enters at the outset by the back door, as it were, and ultimately re-enters at the front, crowned with complete success. The Crawfords enter early and brilliantly, yet are excluded by the time Fanny takes possession. Finally, Sir Thomas's withdrawal and return give rise to the events of the second movement in the same way that Fanny's withdrawal and return accompany those of the third.

The beauty of the structural balance and unity with which the novel traces Fanny's development from alien dependent to presiding judge—from ward to warden—is only as significant as the change of family relations it traces. Mansfield is, at the crisis, maintained by Fanny's moral support of Edmund, after the end of his affair with Mary: "After wandering about and sitting under trees with Fanny all the summer evenings, he had so well talked his

A Reading of *Mansfield Park*

mind into submission, as to be very tolerably cheerful again" (Ch. XLVIII, p. 462). Similarly, Fanny represents nothing less to Sir Thomas than a new daughter to substitute for his lost ones: "Fanny was indeed the daughter that he wanted" (Ch. XLVIII, p. 472). In the same terms, Edmund addresses her as a sister before taking her to wife: " 'My Fanny — my only sister — my only comfort now!' " (Ch. XLVI, p. 444). Mrs. Norris is not entirely mistaken when she gives Fanny's presence as the reason Maria is not eventually allowed to return to Mansfield, for Fanny has displaced both sisters in the family's affections.

The structure of that part of the plot which has to do with Sir Thomas's choice of a new daughter strikes a resonant chord. His is the situation of Lear after his two elder daughters have proved to be harpies. In considering the parallel to Lear's choice of one daughter among three, we are led to Freud's essay on their common prototype, "The Theme of the Three Caskets." Since the essay is not well enough known among literary scholars, it may be desirable to review its complicated argument. Freud begins with the fairy-tale motif of Bassanio's choice among three caskets to win the hand of Portia in *The Merchant of Venice*, and associates it with Lear's choice among his three daughters and with similar tests in a variety of literatures. In widening the reference, he turns to the Cinderella story, bringing the discussion close to the themes of *Mansfield Park*. As he compares the heroines of the classic forms of the tale, Freud observes that they are all hidden and silent: "Cordelia makes herself unrecognizable, inconspicuous like lead, she remains dumb, she 'loves and is silent.' Cinderella hides so that she cannot be found. We may perhaps be allowed to equate concealment and dumbness." [6] He goes on to make the further equation of dumbness and death: the chosen women are usually pale, ethereal creatures whose love has something bloodless, otherworldly, and renunciatory about it. If we accept this thesis, we may be prepared to follow Freud in his most agile imaginative leap: "But if the third of the sisters is the Goddess of Death, the sisters are known to us.

The Structure of the Myth

They are the Fates, the Moerae, the Parcae or the Norns, the third of whom is called Atropos, the inexorable."

At this point the reader impatient with psychoanalytic associationism might object that the third of the daughters, far from being the most macabre of deities, is the most desirable, most loving, even — as in Paris's choice of Aphrodite — most beautiful. Freud acknowledges and speculates on the duality of the chosen one, and finds it at the heart of the Cinderella story: it is eventually the ugliest who is fairest; in *Lear*, it is the coldest who is most loving. The choice which opens greatest possibilities of happiness is precisely the one men seem most to abhor. We are in a better position now to appreciate the irrational hostility which Fanny Price has almost universally evoked: she is at once the most attractive and the most repulsive character in the novel, and the only appropriate response to her is a deeply ambivalent one.

What conclusions are we to draw from our recognition of the inevitable ambivalence toward the chosen one? Freud's interpretation of *Lear* is summary: "Eternal wisdom, clothed in the primeval myth, bids the old man renounce love, choose death and make friends with the necessity of dying." But he had not in this essay of 1913 developed the idea of ambivalence toward death as fully as he was later to do in *Beyond the Pleasure Principle*. There Freud sets out an admittedly "meta-psychological" explanation of those kinds of behavior which cannot be understood as pursuit of pleasure. He redefines pleasure itself as the reduction, or maintenance at a constant level, of psychic and sensory excitation, and suggests that we have instinctual tendencies to reduce sensation from within and without. In this view, the organism tends to return to its origins, finding there a lower level of activity or none at all. That is, the organism tends toward death, in which there is no painful expenditure of energy at all. The attraction to death is itself, paradoxically, a pursuit of pleasure, and conversely, as Freud concludes, "The pleasure principle seems actually to serve the death-instincts." [7]

From this standpoint, the choice of Fanny in the mythic structure of *Mansfield Park* assumes a new importance: it is a choice of a set of life values — or death values, as they may be considered. Lionel Trilling has characterized the novel in similar terms as a critique of the Romantic or Modern values of vitality, personality, and freedom. By contrast he finds it recommending the worth of tradition, enclosure, and peace. The fullest development of this withdrawal from life is, as Trilling sees it, not Fanny but Lady Bertram:

In the person of Lady Bertram [the novel] affirms, with all due irony, the bliss of being able to remain unconscious of the demands of personality (it is a bliss which is a kind of virtue, for one way of being solid, simple, and sincere, is to be a vegetable). It shuts out the world and the judgment of the world. The sanctions upon which it relies are not those of culture, of quality of being, of personality, but precisely those which the new conception of the moral life minimizes, the sanctions of principle, and it discovers in principle the path to the wholeness of the self which is peace.[8]

We are, after considering the ambivalent values implicit in the choice of Fanny, ready to take this insight a step further. The insidious suggestion of the novel is that it is better — i.e., more gratifying — to renounce pleasure than to enjoy it; better to deny vitality than to affirm it; better to die — or live a death-in-life — than to live. Although it is Lady Bertram who embodies this preference as fully as it is possible to do while remaining among the living, it is Fanny Price who is the chief spokesman for life denial. Although she affirms her love for at least two persons, Edmund and her brother William, her typical response is to deny: the theatricals, the courtship of Henry, even her parents. Fanny may not be an acceptable symbol of death itself, but it is her role to deny the pleasures of life in favor of the pleasures of principle, which feel like death. Edmund turns to her only after his love for a vivacious woman is blighted, and he does so resignedly, for one who can love Fanny is ready to embrace death, too.[9]

If the pattern of *Mansfield Park* is the accession of a Cinderella to dominance and if the significance of her victory lies in the conquest of the chief authority at Mansfield by the life-denying values she represents, it remains to see the property itself, the inherited

domain, in its mythic guise. A way of getting at its nature is by
considering the sense of loss and guilt conveyed by the denouement.

The final action, which brings about a reversal of fortune and the
decisive triumph of Fanny, is, from a detached point of view, simply
the elopement of an unhappily married woman — married, indeed,
to a dolt — with her original lover, with whom she is still deeply
in love. Depending on circumstances and personalities, the act might
be pitied or forgiven, in the manner of *The Ring and the Book*.
How curious, even allowing for her moral rigidity, is the language
of Fanny's response to the event:

> Fanny seemed to herself never to have been shocked before.
> There was no possibility of rest. The evening passed, without a
> pause of misery, the night was totally sleepless. She passed only
> from feelings of sickness to shudderings of horror; and from hot
> fits of fever to cold. The event was so shocking, that there were
> moments even when her heart revolted from it as impossible —
> when she thought it could not be. A woman married only six months
> ago, a man professing himself devoted, even *engaged*, to another —
> that other her near relation — the whole family, both families con-
> nected as they were by tie upon tie, all friends, all intimate together!
> — it was too horrible a confusion of guilt, too gross a complication
> of evil, for human nature, not in a state of utter barbarism, to be
> capable of! — yet her judgment told her it was so. (Ch. XLVI, p.
> 441.)

In one respect Fanny is simply a young girl discovering the power
and irrationality of passion; in another, she is normally indignant
at the inconstancy of her own suitor. But what is the source of the
suggestions of incest that lurk in this passage: the "shudderings of
horror" at the families being "all intimate together," the "confusion
of guilt" in eloping with a "near relation" of one's intended? [10]
And what is the meaning of the judgment that descends upon the
guilty ones: a condemnation (as for "barbarism") which literally
excludes Maria from civilized society? She is exiled from England,
dwelling with Mrs. Norris "in another country — remote and private, . . . shut up together with little society" (Ch. XLVIII, p.
465).

The wages of sin — particularly of this sexually charged sin — is, in fact, not death but expulsion: expulsion from Mansfield Park and loss of its newly discovered bliss. Mansfield gains from this event what it had never had, the aura of paradise. As Fanny returns from Portsmouth to come into her own, "the change was from winter to summer. Her eye fell every where on lawns and plantations of the freshest green; and the trees, though not fully clothed, were in that delightful state, when farther beauty is known to be at hand, and when, while much is actually given to the sight, more yet remains for the imagination." (Ch. XLVI, pp. 446–447.) This Eden, it is suggested, is the only heaven we are likely to know — at least the only one Jane Austen can imagine: "With so much true merit and true love, and no want of fortune or friends, the happiness of the married cousins must appear as secure as earthly happiness can be" (Ch. XLVIII, p. 473). Thus situated, Fanny becomes conscious of an ethical possibility lying at the heart of Christian eschatology: "She was, she felt she was, in the greatest danger of being exquisitely happy, while so many were miserable. The evil which brought such good to her!" (Ch. XLVI, p. 443.) The notion of the *felix culpa* is here expressed with evident self-satisfaction by the elect.

This earthly paradise exists, however, at the heart of a fallen world. Though Mansfield may be reckoned a paradise regained, the most potent use of the archetype is reserved for the account of the visit to Sotherton. It is on this occasion that the Crawfords begin to exert their sexual temptation, to universally destructive effect — Henry leading Maria away from her intended and Mary drawing Edmund away from Fanny. The elements of diction and imagery in the scene conspire to convince us that we are not only in the presence of the introduction of evil into the little world of the Mansfield set but also in the presence of an eternal human situation. The imagery includes the setting of the action in an artificially planted "wilderness" (that contemporary landscaping term reverberates widely), enclosed by iron gates which the illicit lovers try to pierce, and insidiously penetrated by serpentining walks where Mary and Edmund lose themselves (Ch. IX, pp. 94–95). The diction includes snatches of dialogue like Julia's refusal to "punish" herself for her sister's "sins" and her feeling that she has been doing

The Structure of the Myth

"penance" by being paired with Mrs. Rushworth (Ch. V, pp. 100–101).

Mansfield begins in the same fallen state as Sotherton, but is redeemed. To save their fallen Eden, the destined inheritors must be bred to a knowledge of sin and suffering, "the consciousness of being born to struggle and endure." They must die to the flesh, renouncing the possibilities of earthly pleasure. Yet whatever reward and punishment they are to know can only be distributed in the earthly world itself, for the novel concludes "without presuming to look forward to a juster appointment hereafter" (Ch. XLVIII, p. 468). The happiness of Fanny and Edmund is as great as earthly happiness can be: that is, it is without vitality, a kind of death. This echo of Christian renunciation is not, however, allowed to become otherworldly, despairing, or ascetic; Jane Austen's acceptance of the world's limitations is expressed in a pragmatic humanism that undertakes to shape this life as best we can.

Mansfield Park is filled with the language of Evangelical eschatology, emphasizing salvation through faith (without specifying the nature of the object of faith) and insisting on its gratuitousness, given the lack of merit in the recipients. The most articulate employment of this language is in the account of Henry Crawford's courtship of Fanny, which fails because he cannot sustain his devotion without immediate reward after "an opening undesigned and unmerited, led him into the way of happiness" (Ch. XLVIII, p. 467). Henry himself uses this language in his appeals to Fanny:

You have some touches of the angel in you, beyond what—not merely beyond what one sees, because one never sees any thing like it—but beyond what one fancies might be. But still I am not frightened. It is not by equality of merit that you can be won. That is out of the question. It is he who sees and worships your merit the strongest, who loves you most devotedly, that has the best right to a return. There I build my confidence. (Ch. XXXIV, p. 344.)

This vision of Fanny is not confined to Henry but is expressed in even more distinctly Biblical terms by Edmund: "Thank God! . . . it seems to have been the merciful appointment of Providence that the heart which knew no guile, should not suffer" (Ch. XLVII,

p. 455). Fanny becomes a synthesis of Cinderella and the Lamb of God: in Mrs. Norris's terms, she is of "the lowest and the last" (Ch. XXIII, p. 221) who are to inherit the earth. It is this quasi-divine potency that causes Mrs. Norris, the personification of the evil spirit, to think of Fanny as "the daemon of the piece" (Ch. XLVII, p. 448); she is indeed the presiding — if not the moving — spirit in the redemption of Mansfield from its fall into darkness. Yet she bears the blessings not of human fulfillment (as Henry Crawford discovers) but of a release from temptation (as Edmund finds).

Of what importance is this archetypal resolution for the life-denying choice of Fanny among the three "sisters"? The tragic burden of the Freudian metapsychology is its suggestion of an inherent unity in the human tendencies toward life and death, pleasure and pain. We may now add the further identity of heaven and earth or, as in *Mansfield Park*, of the redeemed Eden and the fallen world; both poles are objects of our desire and necessities of our condition.[11] The people of Mansfield fall deeply into "guilt and misery" but some, "not greatly in fault themselves," are restored to "tolerable comfort." The final vision of Fanny's Mansfield marks the full ascendancy of the reality principle: it invites us to make friends with the necessity of guilt, misery, and death while holding out the possibilities of a this-worldly salvation — a feeling of peace after the loss of vitality. There is no transcendence, but men can resignedly take possession of an earth that still lies in potentiality about them. Despite its inherent tendency toward death, Mansfield is found to be an earth that renews itself, as Fanny sees in the green spring at her homecoming.

To say that Fanny emerges as the dominant, if not the dynamic, force at Mansfield Park may seem to oversimplify the complex attitudes that the novel has maintained toward her throughout. It is possible to consider her triumph as a qualified one — the achievement of the power to "struggle and endure" without the acquiring of an ethical sanction. Yet there is another line of response, following from the symbolic status of Fanny as child, which is made available to us in the psychology of Carl Jung:

One of the essential features of the child motif is its futurity. The child is potential future. Hence the occurrence of the child motif in the psychology of the individual signifies as a rule an anticipation of future developments, even though at first sight it may seem like a retrospective configuration. . . . It is therefore not surprising that so many of the mythological saviours are child gods. . . . In the individuation process, [the "child" symbol] anticipates the figure that comes from the synthesis of conscious and unconscious elements in the personality. It is therefore a symbol which unites the opposites; a mediator, bringer of healing, that is, one who makes whole. . . . I have called this wholeness that transcends consciousness the "self." The goal of the individuation process is the synthesis of the self.[12]

The figure of Fanny cannot claim all this sanctifying and synthesizing grace: her own personality hardly represents a mature unity of "conscious and unconscious elements." For all our reservations about her, nevertheless, she has a charismatic power that is easier to acknowledge than to explain. We need not hold her up as a divine savior to grant her a function in the novel paralleling the archetypal role of children in many myths and much literature. We have only to think of the heroines of Shakespeare's late romances or some in James's fiction to put Fanny in a perennial tradition of symbolic suggestion. She is the child who inherits the future and justifies the sufferings of the past.

VI

The Novel and Its Tradition

EVER since Sir Walter Scott's 1815 review of *Emma* praised its author for her "art of copying from nature as she really exists in the common walks of life," critics have more or less consciously situated Jane Austen in the great tradition of English realism. But her place in that tradition has rested on no firmer foundation than a sense that her work is "true to life," even while our notion of realism has grown to include virtues other than verisimilitude. In arriving at an estimate of a novel like *Mansfield Park*, we must see it in its tradition to appreciate how unique it is yet how influential its achievements. Such an estimate goes on almost inevitably, in Jane Austen's case, to an attempt to measure the greatness of the artist in the company of her realist peers.

This chapter begins with some of the particulars of *Mansfield Park*'s innovation and influence — primarily in characterization. It then broadens the question of influence to include the novel's affinity with later works in matters of society and ethics. To suggest *Mansfield Park*'s widest implications, however, it will at the last stage be necessary to offer an integrated view of the novel itself. From a synthesis of the partial perspectives of the preceding chapters, a pattern of significance may be approached. The creation of a complex, ambivalent view of the social life of man and of modern society in particular establishes Jane Austen in the classic tradition of European realism.

The most arresting statements about *Mansfield Park*'s position in the canon have been made by Q. D. Leavis in her introduction to a recent edition of the novel.[1] Not content to claim that it is "the most interesting and important of the Austen novels," Mrs. Leavis goes on to say: "*Mansfield Park*, in technique and subject and prose style and in its thoughtful inquiries into human relationships, looks forward to George Eliot and Henry James; so *Mansfield Park* is the first modern novel in England." Yet these claims for its novelty are tempered by considerations of Jane Austen's position in the wake of lady novelists of the late eighteenth century who "provided her with a moralistic tradition — with crude models for those subtle discussions of matrimonial relations, filial obligations, right feeling and so on, which take up a great deal of space in *Mansfield Park*." Though Mrs. Leavis goes on to specify where Jane Austen makes an advance upon these popular novelists — "the attempt to work out a psychological analysis of feeling, which creates a new style" — it is hard to take seriously her assertions of the novel's initiation of a great tradition if one assents in her estimate of the heroine. For Mrs. Leavis, Fanny "is merely the over-delicate, timidly feminine type of heroine who had been evolved by the women novelists," and her closing triumph is presumably to be accounted to circumstance rather than to her own heroism. Yet it is precisely here that the novel's innovative power can most readily be felt.

To see Fanny Price's story as a Cinderella story is to assign *Mansfield Park* a position among the immortal literary legends, but to see its central position in English fiction we must recognize it as a *Bildungsroman* — or, more evocatively, a story of the "young man (or girl) from the provinces." The most important treatments of this theme in the eighteenth century — the novels of Fielding and Smollett — mix moral education with picaresque adventure in such a way that their heroes cannot be said to be educated at all. They simply hear the advice of an Adams or Allworthy, and meanwhile by good fortune and inviolable innocence succeed in doing good for themselves and others. Fanny is the first young person (if we discount, each in her way, Pamela and Clarissa) who learns enough of the world to win through to success by moral effort. After her stretches a line of morally resourceful heroines from Jeanie Deans to Maggie Verver. Moral effort is in her not simply a rigid adherence to the principles of a previous education, but in itself an educative process. Fanny learns the attractiveness of Henry Crawford and the mercenariness of Sir Thomas; she learns not only the alien disorder of her parents' home but the flaw at the heart of Mansfield. Fanny is the first English heroine we can observe in the process of coming to know the moral world.

If we seek, therefore, her immediate literary descendants we have not far to go to the outraged orphans in the novels of Dickens, from Oliver to Pip. It has also been noted in passing (e.g., by W. A. Craik) that Fanny's situation in several respects resembles that of Jane Eyre. Literally an orphan, Jane is adopted by as harsh and unsympathetic an aunt as Mrs. Norris. Though playing a Cinderella role throughout her life, she, too, eventually wins the heart of the master of the house. Like Fanny, Jane is attached to an idealistic clergyman, an attachment in which moral admiration is predominant over sexual attraction. The vast difference between the novels is that Jane's sexual vibration far exceeds Fanny's faint stirrings for Henry Crawford. Fanny remains true to Edmund, though aware of Henry's sexual charm; although idealistically attracted to St. John Rivers, Jane finally fulfills her vitality with Rochester. Despite this important difference of sensibility, however, *Jane Eyre* stands among the progeny of *Mansfield Park* by its sustained focus on the young girl from the provinces finding her way through the world, experiencing the inner drama of moral and sexual impulses, and overcoming her limitations — both internal and external — through a sustained exercise of moral will that makes her a heroine. For all Charlotte Brontë's distaste for an author to whom "the passions are perfectly unknown," she is of the tribe of Jane.

If her relation to her counterparts in earlier and later English *Bildungsromanen* were not sufficient to establish Fanny's crucial position as a literary type, her standing among other Austen heroines would do so. She has so often been unfavorably compared with her predecessor, Elizabeth Bennet, that it has somehow escaped notice that she is a more complex and changeful character than that charming heroine. Elizabeth Bennet is the fruition of a traditional type, not the first example of a new one. She is endowed both with the wit of eighteenth-century heroines and with their animal vitality: she is Sophia Western grown up. And it is impossible for the novelist to go further in this direction. Elizabeth Bennet does not develop in *Pride and Prejudice*; she merely changes her mind — but it is the same lively and healthy mind throughout. It would be difficult to find in English letters after her a hero or heroine who is both healthy and interesting.

Fanny, too, is the fruition of a traditional type — not that of Sophia Western but that of Clarissa Harlowe. Fanny's mind, like Clarissa's, is a psychic jungle, and it is curious that modern readers have found her less interesting, as well as less attractive, than that saintly sufferer. Modern taste strongly inclines us to follow the conscience's journey through darkness, and most of the major nineteenth-century novelists were similarly inclined. Whereas Elizabeth Bennet ends a century, Fanny Price begins one. Her spiritual sisters, to name only the high points of the tradition, are Dorothea Brooke, Amelia Osborne, Lucy Feverel, and Sue Bridehead. Without making invidious comparisons, it is safe to say that all maintain a high moral ideal strongly colored by personal motives, and are led, by their experience of the social world, either to tragedy or to the development of a subtler ethic.

What distinguishes these young women is not alone their inadequate means of coping with their precarious or unprotected states, but also their discovery of the rigors of social survival for the isolated self. They come into the world with strong expectations not so much of happiness as of living according to their ideal conceptions of themselves, and either the world assigns them an inimical situation or, through their personal imbalance, they choose such a situation for themselves. It is above all their idealism — however different its forms — that binds them to an image of themselves they cannot realize in their nineteenth-century setting. *Mansfield Park* is, after *Clarissa*, the first of the great English novels to show how the life of the individual is created by the action on the open self of the social groups — and their representative individuals — which make up its world.

Society may be defined for Jane Austen as a system of interdependence, in which the social world and the self are the participants. If she has any moral intention at all it is to enforce the ultimacy of our connections by exhibiting the loneliness of those men and women who fail to recognize them, e.g., in the false claim of freedom of sensibility by Marianne Dashwood, and in the false claim of freedom of imagination by Emma Woodhouse. The instruments of enhancing or maintaining these relations are the manners and morals of any society, together with the will to use them effectively in creating that uniquely human goal, the fulfillment of the self — of which marriage is the highest form in Jane Austen.

Nor must the individual's response to society be passive or acquiescent. One intention of *Mansfield Park* is to set up ways of modifying the manners and morals of the beau monde of London and of the gentry at Mansfield. It aims, that is, to refine the kinds of value judgment which these societies themselves employ. The novel does this by showing the members of the country gentry some of the inadequacies of their own moral and religious tradition, while proposing their enrichment through incorporating certain values of Romanticism and Evangelicalism. In addition, it demonstrates how real and indispensable is the individual's connection with society and its representative personalities by criticizing the belief in their own independence which almost all the characters cherish.

In affirming the abiding reality of society, *Mansfield Park* resembles no other novel so much as it does a modern work, perhaps the last of the tradition that firmly maintains this attitude. E. M. Forster's *Howards End*, almost a hundred years later, takes up the condition of the gentry roughly where Jane Austen left it. As Lionel Trilling has said of *Howards End*, it is "a novel about England's fate" which "asks the question, 'Who shall inherit England?' " [2] The same may be said of *Mansfield Park*. Both novels take their titles from the names of country places; both are suggestively ambivalent in their treatment of the gentry; both have as their theme an attitude expressed in the epigraph of *Howards End*: "Only connect . . ." This theme is elaborated by Forster in the words, "Only connect, and the beast and the monk, robbed of the isolation that is life to either, will die," [3] and in *Mansfield Park* in the words of Mary Crawford to Fanny, "I feel that we are born to be connected" (Ch. XXXVI, p. 359). Both tales hinge on class divisions that make personal relations difficult or impossible,[4] and both envision the ideal of human connection in symbolic terms.[5] In these respects the two novels stand near the beginning and the end of a line of works that runs through *Vanity Fair*, *Middlemarch*, and *Tess of the D'Urbervilles*.

It is worthwhile now to consider one further judgment by Mary Lascelles, for it not only summarizes the theme of connection in *Mansfield Park* but suggests terms for deciding the novel's proper genre:

In the earlier novels, all those indefinable sympathies and antipathies which, like filaments, connect people whom kinship or fortune associates, occasionally threaten to be resolved into likes and dislikes, or even reduced to the simpler terms of approval and disapproval. These sympathies and antipathies have been adroitly complicated by misunderstandings; but such misunderstanding of the character and conduct of other people is simple compared with the Bertrams' and Crawfords' misunderstanding of the nature of their relationships, one to another and each to himself. For . . . *Mansfield Park* is a comedy, with grave implications, of human interdependence numbly unrealized or wilfully ignored until too late.[6]

In these words, the novel's theme — human connection threatened by misunderstanding and antipathy — is related to the aesthetics of comedy, whose roots lie deep in the affirmation of social norms.

Jane Austen's power as a comic artist has usually been discussed as it is manifested in *Pride and Prejudice* (or *Emma*). Several critics have shown that the novel's comedy depends on its ordered dialectic, in which the classical values of character and reason in Darcy and the romantic values of personality and emotion in Elizabeth are criticized, modified, and finally united when they marry. It is true that *Mansfield Park* is not so purely comic as *Pride and Prejudice*, for it lacks that novel's beautiful progressive structure. Yet it has more such beauty than has hitherto been supposed. Much the same dialectic goes on in *Mansfield Park*, except that the final synthesis is thwarted, not by the author's lack of comic vision but by the difference in the characters she has chosen as her subjects. When we distinguish the two novels in this way we no longer see them as opposed but rather as elucidating the same problems by means of different situations and arriving at appropriate conclusions. As Reuben Brower has pithily put it, "the ambiguities in Jane Austen do not multiply indefinitely. Tracing them does not merely give us a headache but leads to a precise outlining of the alternatives and to a practical resolution." [7]

With these possibilities in mind, we recognize the difficulty of a final appraisal of the achievement of *Mansfield Park*. If the synthesis toward which it points is incomplete within it, can we call it as great as the coherently developed work of art Jane Austen was able to make of *Pride and Prejudice*? The problem is something like the one involved in calling either the *Inferno* or the *Paradiso* the greater — the one with its stronger moral force, the other with its vision of moral harmony. But we do not judge parts of Dante's poem in this way, and perhaps we can arrive at a final judgment of these two novels only by taking into account their place in the Austen canon. We will then see them in a sequence of meaning, refining a subject essentially the same, and progressively unfolding the forms it assumes in human society.

"Let other pens dwell on guilt and misery." When we turn at last to the famous words with which Jane Austen begins the last chapter and its weary summary of the denouement, we face the question, what is *Mansfield Park*'s vision of the world, as represented by the end of the novel? In the words "guilt and misery" the authorial voice seems to be talking about the events of illness and elopement which have just shaken the ordered society from its complacent slumbers. But her wider reference is to the novel as a whole, which traces the omissions and imperfections of its characters to their final issue in guilt and misery. Nevertheless, the last chapter manages to salvage, if it cannot save, the ideal of a viable society in the muted celebration of the marriage of Fanny and Edmund. The one constant in Jane Austen's investigation is that society endures; it seems to be the only immortal being to which we can attach ourselves. This ultimate, though limited, faith in the value of human society preserves *Mansfield Park* for comedy.

Jane Austen here as elsewhere distributes rewards and punishments within the compass of an imperfect world, "without pretending to look forward to a juster appointment hereafter." Though she does not give us in this novel a vision of human happiness at its grandest — the kind of happiness she can conceive of in *Persuasion* — she presents the marriage of Edmund and Fanny as a happiness that "must appear as secure as earthly happiness can be." But this security — like the economic and social position of the Bertrams and their class — depends on the human will to accept an imperfect world, on the human effort which practices as well as preaches clerical and other reforms, and on the human skill in shoring up a class's moral life to face historical change. At every level — psychological, mythic, and social — the vision of *Mansfield Park* is humanistic. It squarely acknowledges the imperfection of its historical situation while maintaining the secular hope that was to animate the nineteenth century. This mixture of negation and affirmation is the most consistent feature of *Mansfield Park* and may be said to be its pattern of dramatic implication — what has often been broadly termed its comic irony.

The reduction to a pattern of so rich a fabric as *Mansfield Park* would be scarcely desirable even if it were possible. Yet the result of seeing the object from several points of view is to reach for some synthesis that will take in the sum — and perhaps more — of what is seen. Given the preceding three chapters' conclusions about social theme, character, and mythos or plot, what common principle can be said to control the novel's dramatic working in every part? The characteristic form of Jane Austen's treatment of social classes, as it has emerged in this study, is a mingling of commitment to the gentry's fortunes with her determined refusal to become a partisan. Although restricting her views largely to her own class, she censures it at least as much as she does the aristocracy — and for similar reasons. Her object being not missionary but corrective, her judgment of Mansfield Park must be ambivalent. In the working out of the plot she reckons strengths and weaknesses, and estimates dangers; she is committed and detached at the same time.

Similarly, in the treatment of character, ambivalence or irony rules. Fanny is presented as an inextricable knot of moral idealism and self-protective egoism, and — to convince us of the binding power of the knot — we are struck by the directness with which a high moral standard is put in the service of self-protection. Again, as in evaluating social classes, partisan slogans are much less useful than double vision in forming conclusions about Fanny. She is like Mansfield Park itself in her stuffiness and mediocrity, and the mingled boredom and awe with which we are to regard the place are equally due the person.

Finally, the same balance of attitudes must be maintained in considering the peculiar twist given to the Cinderella fable by the plot of *Mansfield Park*. The heroine is rewarded for long suffering by triumphing over her persecutors and inheriting (or effectively controlling) the family estate. But the realm inherited proves to be a fallen Eden limited by moral and religious imperfections and threatened with dissolution by economic and political forces it seems too weak to resist. We are to see Fanny and Edmund as the best available people to dominate Mansfield Park from their position in the rectory, but not as the ideal — the novel itself has envisioned better marriages than theirs, marriages in which the Crawfords' vitality is controlled by their sobriety. In coming into control of Mansfield, Fanny and Edmund establish the same ambivalent pattern in the plot as exists in the social theme and character study.

To what end do these parallel ambivalences work: do they neutralize the force of the novel by passive acceptance or detached irony? Beyond the social program which might be deduced for the gentry, and beyond the moral insight we may gain from the study of Fanny's psychology, *Mansfield Park* offers a vision of reality which is, to my knowledge, unprecedented in English fiction but which becomes the dominant note of the nineteenth-century novel. Nineteenth-century English realism is the tradition founded by Jane Austen, by virtue of her steady grasp of human imperfection, her heroic commitment to a world riddled with personal aggression — and touched occasionally by love.

To substantiate the claim that Jane Austen's realism is something more than common-sense verisimilitude,[8] we may examine a passage in which her special vision of reality is at work. After Edmund has described to Fanny his parting scene with Mary Crawford, the following appears:

Fanny, now at liberty to speak openly, felt more than justified in adding to his knowledge of her real character, by some hint of what share his brother's state of health might be supposed to have in her wish for a complete reconciliation. This was not an agreeable intimation. Nature resisted it for a while. It would have been a vast deal pleasanter to have had her more disinterested in her attachment; but his vanity was not of a strength to fight long against reason. He submitted to believe, that Tom's illness had influenced her; only reserving for himself this consoling thought, that considering the many counteractions of opposing habits, she had certainly been *more* attached to him than could have been expected, and for his sake been more near doing right. Fanny thought exactly the same; and they were also quite agreed in their opinion of the lasting effect, the indelible impression, which such a disappointment must make on his mind. Time would undoubtedly abate somewhat of his sufferings, but still it was a sort of thing which he never could get entirely the better of; and as to his ever meeting with any other woman who could — it was too impossible to be named but with indignation. Fanny's friendship was all that he had to cling to. (Ch. XLVII, pp. 459–460.)

A complete analysis of these sentences, revealing the play of unconscious motives and implicit communications, would demand the precision and amplitude of an *explication de texte*. The attention they give to the minute and evanescent in personal feelings is in the best tradition of realism, but it could have been accomplished by Richardson or even Fanny Burney. What marks this passage as new in the development of realism is its awareness of human brutality. To put it baldly, Fanny is telling the brokenhearted Edmund that his lost love wanted him only for his money. This is aggression not only against her defeated rival but against her reluctant lover. Edmund, in his own bitterness after rejection, consents to the impugning of Mary's motives, even at the cost of relinquishing his belief in her love: "his vanity was not of a strength to fight long against reason" (reverse the terms to reveal the truth). But he amply revenges himself against Fanny by expanding on his eternal devotion to Mary and by scorning a substitute — for Fanny, he reminds her, is his only "friend."

Once we are aware of the ambivalence pervading the novel, it becomes impossible to believe that Jane Austen's treatment of this couple reduces them either to heroes or to villains. Her triumph is greater: she bathes them in the hard, undeviating light of realism and yet preserves them as human beings. After Jane Austen's novels, long before Sartre conceived of the *regard*,[9] the stare by which men mentally annihilate each other as a pre-condition of their own freedom, a series of major writers unveiled the hostility — indeed, the sadism — in most personal relations. The realistic novelists saw clearly that only by negating the individuality of others and reducing them to objects do we protect our own individuality. Or, in Brecht's dictum: "What keeps a man alive? He feeds on others." If this war of ego is carried on by each against all, society is indeed as Hobbes described it, *bellum omnia in omnes*. Yet for Jane Austen the amazing fact about this struggle is its constancy and continuity: society is permanent organized hostility, and for better or worse it is the only permanence we can attain.

This clear-sighted view of the horror of social intercourse serves to modify Jane Austen's affirmation of the social world as the setting of all human values. Herein lies the most inclusive of the ambivalences which we have seen operating in every aspect of *Mansfield Park*. What Austen critics have persistently spoken of as irony

— both the satirical and revelatory sorts — is perhaps at bottom this mixed feeling about social life. Society is, for Jane Austen, both the horizon of our possibilities and the arena where we destroy each other. In this double vision of the life of man in society, she stands within the imaginative movement that stretches from Laclos through Balzac to Proust. This movement of mind can be considered one of the dominant strains in Western culture since 1789,[10] and by participating in it *Mansfield Park* becomes a classic in the literature of modern Western culture.

NOTES

Notes

Preface

1 Two recent articles are cases in point: Joseph W. Donohue, Jr., "Ordination and the Divided House at Mansfield Park," *ELH*, XXXII (1965), 169–178; and Thomas R. Edwards, Jr., "The Difficult Beauty of *Mansfield Park*," *Nineteenth-Century Fiction*, XX (1965), 51–67.

I. *Introduction: The Whole Novel*

1 My discussion of "perspectivism" centers on Ortega's version of this approach because his is most closely tied to aesthetic problems and to the novel in particular. José Ferrater Mora, *Ortega y Gasset: An Outline of His Philosophy* (London, 1956), pp. 25–37, mentions exponents of perspectivism as various as Nietzsche, Vaihinger, and Russell, but its main stream seems to run parallel to the phenomenological school. (Literary critics have also used the term, e.g., René Wellek and Austin Warren, *Theory of Literature* (New York, 1956 [1949], pp. 145 *et passim*, in the course of a discussion of the metaphysical status of literary works that draws heavily on the phenomenology of Roman Ingarden.) Despite my interest in the phenomenological "bracketing" of the aesthetic object as a created structure with an existence and coherence of its own, I remain unsatisfied by the application of this quasi-new-critical principle to the reading of fiction. As will be seen in the discussion below of the place of scientific evidence in interpreting fictional worlds, it does not accord with the novel's dense texture and evocation of a lived universe to continually remind ourselves of its artificiality. Despite his protestations of maintaining aesthetic distance from the world portrayed in fiction ("On Point of View in the Arts"), Ortega manages to communicate a sense of his immersion in the human facts conveyed by fiction — which makes me prefer him to the more pure phenomenologists.

2 *The Dehumanization of Art and Other Writings on Art and Culture*

A Reading of *Mansfield Park*

(Garden City, N.Y., 1956), p. 95. For a keen analysis of the metaphysical basis of Ortega's "derealized" fictional world, see W. J. Harvey, *Character and the Novel* (Ithaca, N.Y., 1965), pp. 211–217.

My own view here will be rather more "kinetic" than Ortega's "aesthetic" one (to use Joyce's terms) — a reading of the novel as "mimetic" not "autonomous" (to use Harvey's). I have never resolved the philosophic cruxes of the theories of realistic imitation and aesthetic ideality, but my recent thinking on the subject revolves around a passage in Freud's "The Relation of the Poet to Day-Dreaming" (*The Standard Edition of the Complete Psychological Works of Sigmund Freud*, James Strachey, ed. [London, 1958], IX, 152–153). After proposing that daydreams are wishes and poets daydreamers, he concludes with a characteristic idea: ". . . the essential *ars poetica* lies in the technique of overcoming the feeling of repulsion in us which is undoubtedly connected with the barriers that rise between each single ego and the others. We can guess two of the methods used by this technique. The writer softens the character of his egoistic day-dreams by altering and disguising it, and he bribes us by the purely formal — that is, aesthetic — yield of pleasure which he offers us in the presentation of his phantasies."

ii. *The Novel among the Critics*

1 Letter of Anne Romilly to Maria Edgeworth, quoted in Charles B. Hogan, "Jane Austen and Her Early Public," *Review of English Studies*, n.s., I (1950), 43.

2 H. W. Garrod, "Jane Austen: A Depreciation," *Essays by Divers Hands*, n.s., VIII (1928), 37.

3 Barbara B. Collins, "Jane Austen's Victorian Novel," *Nineteenth-Century Fiction*, IV (1949), 175–185.

4 Leonard Woolf, "The Economic Determinism of Jane Austen," *New Statesman and Nation*, n.s., XXIV (1942), 39–41; David Daiches, "Jane Austen, Karl Marx, and the Aristocratic Dance," *American Scholar*, XVII (1947–48), 289–296.

5 Marvin Mudrick, *Jane Austen: Irony as Defense and Discovery* (Princeton, 1952), Ch. VI, "The Triumph of Gentility: *Mansfield Park*"; e.g., "The thesis of *Mansfield Park* is severely moral: that one world, representing the genteel orthodoxy of Jane Austen's time, is categorically superior to any other. . . . To this thesis, everything else gives way: in the end, it subordinates or destroys every character; the function of the heroine is to ensure its full acceptance." (P. 155.) See also Kingsley Amis, "What Became of Jane Austen? *Mansfield Park*," *Spectator*, CIC (1957), 439–440; e.g., "What became of that Jane Austen (if she ever existed) who set out bravely to correct conventional notions of the desirable and virtuous? From being their critic (if she ever was) she became their slave. That is another way of saying that her judgment and her moral sense were corrupted. *Mansfield Park* is the witness of that corruption." (P. 440.)

6 Andrew H. Wright, *Jane Austen's Novels: A Study in Structure* (London, 1953), p. 60. Edd Winfield Parks writes in the same vein: "It is her only book in which all the resolution is by authorial explanation. Dramatic interplay of character upon character disappears, while the author presents her decisions in a surprisingly argumentative tone"; "Exegesis in Jane Austen's Novels," *South Atlantic Quarterly*, LI (1952), 116.

Notes

7 Mary Lascelles, "Some Characteristics of Jane Austen's Style," *Essays and Studies,* XXII (1937), 76–77.

8 Lionel Trilling, "*Mansfield Park,*" *The Opposing Self: Nine Essays in Criticism* (New York, 1955), p. 210. This position has recently been restated in A. Walton Litz, *Jane Austen: A Study of Her Artistic Development* (New York, 1965), and, in another form, in W. A. Craik, *Jane Austen: The Six Novels* (London, 1965).

9 Donald J. Greene, "Jane Austen and the Peerage," *PMLA,* LXVIII (1953), 1017–1031. The quotation below is from page 1029.

10 Arnold Kettle, *An Introduction to the English Novel,* 2 vols. (New York and Evanston, 1960 [1951]), I, 99 ff.

11 *The Political Ideas of the English Romanticists* (London, etc., 1926), p. 107. For the primary texts of the Romantics' political thinking, with an introduction adumbrating the thesis presented here, see R. J. Write, ed., *Political Tracts of Wordsworth, Coleridge and Shelley* (Cambridge, 1953).

12 *Jane Austen: Letters to Her Sister Cassandra and Others,* R. W. Chapman, ed., 2 vols. (Oxford, 1932), II, 297. (The date is January 29, 1813, well along in the writing of the novel.) This collection will subsequently be cited parenthetically with an abbreviated title *Letters; Mansfield Park* will be parenthetically cited, without title. The edition used is the standard modern one by R. W. Chapman, but my references to chapter numbers are altered to conform to editions without division into volumes; the page number following is that of the third Chapman edition (Oxford, 1948 [1923]).

III. *The Novel in Its Time*

1 "The Ordinations in Jane Austen's Novels," *Nineteenth-Century Fiction,* X (1955–56), 156–159. The technicalities of the canons are best left in Branton's words:

"The ancient (and also modern) canons of the Church require that ordinations be held on the Sundays following the Ember weeks, and if for urgent reasons it be found necessary for a bishop to ordain at some other time, that he obtain special dispensation from the Archbishop of Canterbury. The canons also require that a candidate for the priesthood spend a year in the office of deacon before he is admitted to the office of priest. . . .

". . . On December 23 'he [Edmund] was going to a friend near Peterborough in the same situation as himself, and they were to receive ordination in the course of the Christmas week.' Edmund plans to be gone only a week, although he does stay away longer visiting friends. When he returns, we find that he 'had already gone through the service once since his ordination' and must have entered upon his clerical duties right away. The service was doubtless morning or evening prayer rather than the Communion service, and Edmund might have read it even if he had been only in deacon's orders, but the impression given is that he is a priest.

"His ordination, moreover, probably did not occur on the canonical day, since the date of the first Sunday following the December Ember days is never later than December 24, and had his ordination taken place on that date, Jane Austen would doubtless have said that he was to receive ordination on the following day, rather than 'in the course of the Christmas week.'

. . . .

"We may wonder how to account for the irregularities in Jane Austen's ordinations. It is possible that Jane, like her heroine Elinor, knew so little of the technicalities of the subject that she simply made mistakes, but since she professed to write only about what she knew and since she was the daughter and sister of clergymen, that possibility seems unlikely. It seems more probable that she was reflecting the actual practice of her day, even though ecclesiastical histories of the period have little to say about these particular abuses, and that her novels are more reliable guides to the period so far as the customs and practices of the lesser gentry are concerned than are the specialized histories."

2 Q. D. Leavis, "A Critical Theory of Jane Austen's Writings," *Scrutiny*, X, 114 ff. *Pace* Mrs. Leavis, the evidence for Jane Austen's Evangelical tendencies is strangely inconsistent. The clergymen in her family exhibited both the abuses and the higher standards of conduct which the Evangelicals took up: her father was guilty of pluralism (though his parishes were only a mile apart), but her brother James refused a second living, believing that to take it would constitute simony. Though in 1809 she baldly declared, "I do not like the Evangelicals" (*Letters*, I, 265), in 1814 we find her writing, "I am by no means convinced that we ought not all to be Evangelicals" (*Letters*, II, 410). By 1816, however, her taste had turned again: "We do not much like Mr. Cooper's new Sermons; — they are fuller of Regeneration and Conversion than ever — with the addition of his zeal in the cause of the Bible Society" (*Letters*, II, 467). On this sort of evidence we can assume only that she was open to the moral reformism of the movement yet contemptuous of its indecorous enthusiasm. Hers is the enlightened gentry's attitude, which Crabbe, for one, expresses in *The Parish Register* (Jane Austen's source of Fanny Price's name and character): the "slumbering priest" and the emotional revivalist are both targets for satire.

3 The denouement is typical of a period during which economic change wrought a transformation in the material position of the clergy. Prosperous agriculture enhanced stipends, and the social status of the clergy rose, parallel to the growing refinement of the gentry. See Kenneth MacLean, *Agrarian Age: A Background for Wordsworth* (New Haven and London, 1950), *passim*.

4 Elie Halévy, *A History of the English People in the Nineteenth Century*, E. I. Watkin and D. A. Barker, trans. (New York, 1961), I, 359 ff.

5 The distribution of these material rewards of virtue reflects the tendency toward increased worldliness in this period. As their resistance to higher stipends for curates suggests, the holders of livings were thoroughly dedicated to the attempt to emulate the standards of the class with which they identified themselves, the gentry. Newman's judgment of Jane Austen's worldly clergymen is typical: "what vile creatures her parsons are! she has not a dream of the high Catholic *ethos*." (Newman was, however, not only a devoted Janeite but is reported to have read *Mansfield Park* every year, "in order to perfect and preserve his style.") Cited in Charles F. Harrold, *John Henry Newman: An Expository and Critical Study of His Mind, Thought• and Art* (London, New York, and Toronto, 1945), p. 421.

6 This, Halévy's influential thesis, is borne out by recent historical research. The widespread immorality of the aristocracy at the end of the eighteenth century, and particularly its many personal connections with the still scarcely respectable theatrical world, are set out in David Spring, "Aristocracy, Social Structure, and Religion in the Early Victorian Period," *Victo-*

Notes

rian Studies, VI (1962–63), 263–280. Spring describes the changes wrought in the upper classes by Evangelical fervor, including the refusal of some of the younger zealots to watch private theatricals. He accounts for the religious revival by the general leveling of society, the rise to social prominence of professional and mercantile families who challenged the standards of morality and religion of their erstwhile betters.

7 William Reitzel, "*Mansfield Park* and *Lovers' Vows*," *Review of English Studies*, IX (1933), 451–456. See also E. M. Butler, "*Mansfield Park* and Kotzebue's 'Lovers' Vows,'" *Modern Language Review*, XXVIII (1933), 326–337; H. Winifred Husbands, "'Mansfield Park' and 'Lovers' Vows': A Reply," *Modern Language Review*, XXIX (1934), 176 ff.; Sybil Rosenfeld, "Jane Austen and Private Theatricals," *Essays and Studies*, 1962, pp. 40–51; David Lodge, "A Question of Judgment: The Theatricals at Mansfield Park," *Nineteenth-Century Fiction*, XVII (1962), 275–282. Convenient summaries of the plot are given in Litz, *op. cit.*, p. 123, and in Brinton, *op. cit.*, p. 39.

8 Hannah More's *Moral Sketches*, for example, attacked the tendency in contemporary literature to make the seducer appealing and thereby inspire the reader to imitation. Tales (cf. *Clarissa*) and dramas of seduction were admissible, however, if they took the conventional sentimentalist view of the seduced girl as tainted, though pathetic. But when, as in *Lovers' Vows*, she was the innocent victim not only of the seducer but of his class, the aristocracy, such literature became politically dangerous.

9 Home was also politically suspect as a libertarian: he speaks the language of liberty in dedicating *Douglas* to the Prince of Wales (later George III): "The envied State of this Nation cannot remain precisely as it is; the Tide must flow, or ebb faster than it has ever flowed." It is as a victim of authoritarian persecution that Mrs. Inchbald, the adapter of *Lovers' Vows*, describes Home in her anthology, *The British Theatre* . . . (London, 1808), XVI, 5 ("Remarks" on *Douglas*). The play does not, of course, express radical sentiments, although it hints at Scotch nationalist ones, which might then have been construed as rebellious.

10 R. W. Chapman suggests the view developed here: "The class to which Jane Austen . . . belonged regarded the aristocracy with suspicious hostility. Now *Lovers' Vows* was under that cloud; it was introduced by an Hon. John Yates . . . from a country-house performance the cast of which had included a duke. But dukes as a class, and baronets and country parsons as a class, were then remote from each other; the former class despised its inferiors, and the inferiors retorted with moral reprobation." (*Jane Austen: Facts and Problems* [Oxford, 1949], pp. 198–199.)

Yates is the younger son of a lord "with a tolerable independence," but "Sir Thomas would probably have thought his introduction at Mansfield by no means desirable" (Ch. XIII, p. 121). When they do meet, Sir Thomas is annoyed by Yates's pursuit of the theatrical project, but his distaste exceeds his normal, measured response: "Mr. Yates's family and connections were sufficiently known to him, to render his introduction as the 'particular friend,' another of the hundred particular friends of his son, exceedingly unwelcome . . ." (Ch. XIX, p. 183). Yates does not directly contribute to the debauchery and illness of Tom, but his eloping with Julia is treated as a loss of status for her, until "there was comfort in finding his estate rather more, and his debts much less, than [Sir Thomas] had feared . . ." (Ch. XLVIII, p. 462). It is not Yates's relative poverty that Sir Thomas fears but his profligacy: "Such was his opinion of the set into which she had thrown herself" (Ch. XLVII, p. 452).

11 *The Poetical Works of William Wordsworth*, E. De Selincourt, ed. (Oxford, 1952 [1944]), II, 389.

12 See Allardyce Nicoll, *A History of Late Eighteenth Century Drama: 1750–1800* (Cambridge, 1927), *passim*. Crane Brinton sums up the play's values in selecting it as a prime instance of Romantic revolt: "Rank is a source of evil. Pride in rank leads us to disown natural acts, and to treat them as if they were unnatural. If the baron had in his youth married the girl he loved in spite of class prejudices, if he had followed his affections and his conscience, instead of his lying reason, the evil in which we see him involved would never have occurred. Society — cultivated society — is always wrong. The individual who has courage to act against it is always right." (*Op. cit.*, p. 39.)

13 Quoted in Reitzel, *op. cit.*, p. 453. Kotzebue later became a hero of the conservative press after he was assassinated, apparently in revenge for his political conversion; see Brinton, *op. cit.*, p. 214.

14 *The Collected Works of William Hazlitt*, A. R. Waller and Arnold Glover, eds. (London and New York, 1902), V, 360.

15 See Frank W. Bradbrook, "Sources of Jane Austen's Ideas about Nature in 'Mansfield Park,'" *Notes and Queries*, n.s., CCVI (1961), 222-224, where the Romantic character of Fanny's taste is related to its sources in Anne Radcliffe's descriptions of Italian landscape, Wordsworth's picture of Tintern Abbey, and William Gilpin's version of the picturesque. I regret that I have been able to examine neither Mr. Bradbrook's recent book nor that of David Lodge, whose article is cited above.

16 Charles Murrah, "The Background of *Mansfield Park*," in *From Jane Austen to Joseph Conrad*, Robert C. Rathburn and Martin Steinmann, Jr., eds. (Minneapolis, 1958), pp. 23-34.

17 Reuben A. Brower, in his introduction to the Riverside edition of *Mansfield Park* (Boston, 1965), considers the "climactic scene" of the novel to be the change of Sir Thomas's attitude toward Fanny after she rejects Henry Crawford; her acceptance into the family, marked by the provision of a fire for her comfort, seems to imply his conversion from mannered decorum to moral delicacy. This leaves out of account the possibility that Fanny's standing with Sir Thomas improves as soon as he knows she is sought by a man with £4,000 a year. Brower does, however, conclude that "there are enough ironic vibrations in the air both before and after the scene to keep us from confusing Sir Thomas with the fairy godmother of the piece" (p. xxi).

18 It is well known that Crabbe was one of Jane Austen's favorite poets; even at Mansfield, his volume of verse *Tales* is, anachronistically, being read (Ch. XVI, p. 156). Crabbe's Fanny (the daughter of a bailiff) is an innocent offspring of the middle class pursued by the rakish Sir Edward Archer ("Maidens chaste and lovely shun his sight"). He offers her attractions much in the manner of Don Giovanni — pointing out, as Keats's almost contemporary lines have it, that

> Love in a hut, with water and a crust
> Is — Love forgive us! — cinders, ashes, dust.

To this Fanny opposes the ideal of her parents' marriage — to be poor but honest. This ideal is made to prevail, as Fanny marries her "peasant" beau

Notes

and Sir Edward's conscience moves him to further their happiness. It is this Romantic image of innocent mediocrity that is upheld in *Mansfield Park* as well.

19 The precise dating of the action is subject to the limitations of any literalist approach to a fictional world. R. W. Chapman has proposed that Jane Austen used an almanac; that the only full date given in the novel could have occurred, shortly before composition, in 1808; and that "it is natural to suppose that she used almanacs of 1808 and 1809" (appendix to his edition of *Mansfield Park*, p. 553). A. Walton Litz believes that the calendars of 1796–97 are more appropriate because the date of Easter, 1797, corresponds to that "indicated" [sic] in the novel. The text itself gives us this chronology.

Approximate Date	Event	Chapter, Page, and Phrase
1781	Sir Thomas Bertram marries Maria Ward	I, 3: "About thirty years ago" (composition began in 1811)
1787	Rev. Norris marries the second Miss Ward and Lieutenant Price marries Frances Ward	I, 3: "at the end of half a dozen years"
1787–98	No contact between Prices and Mansfield Park	I, 4: "By the end of eleven years"; I, 5: Fanny is "a girl now nine years old"
1799	Fanny comes to Mansfield	II, 12: "Fanny Price was at this time just ten years old"
1804	Rev. Norris dies	III, 23: "the death of Mr. Norris, which happened when Fanny was about fifteen"
1805	Sir Thomas and Tom go to Antigua	III, 32: "These opinions [about Rev. Norris's successor] had been hardly canvassed a year, before another event arose"
September, 1806	Tom returns, Sir Thomas delayed	IV, 37–38: "when September came, Sir Thomas was still abroad . . . Tom arrived safely"
Winter, 1807	Rushworth courts Maria	IV, 38: "The return of winter engagements . . . the introduction of a young man"
July, 1807	Henry and Mary Crawford arrive	IV, 40: "Such was the state of affairs in the month of July, and Fanny had just reached her eighteenth year"
September, 1807	Tom initiates theatricals	XII, 114: "Sir Thomas was to return in November . . . by the end of August, [Tom] arrived himself"

A Reading of *Mansfield Park*

Before November, 1807	Sir Thomas returns early	XIX, 178: "His business in Antigua had latterly been prosperously rapid"

The remainder of the novel's chronology is given by Chapman (pp. 553–556). What I wish to establish here is that by internal evidence the Antigua voyage could not have begun much earlier than 1805 nor ended much later than 1807 — this was precisely the time when the economic depression was setting in. If we take the "thirty years" deduction from 1814, the date of publication, the trip is likely to have occurred in 1808–10, just at the time of the abolition crisis.

20 See L. J. Ragatz, *The Fall of the Planter Class in the British Caribbean, 1763–1833: A Study in Social and Economic History* (New York and London, 1928); also W. J. Burn, *The British West Indies* (London, etc., 1951).

21 An excellent term used in James M. Duffy, Jr., "Moral Integrity and Moral Anarchy in *Mansfield Park*," *ELH*, XXII (1956), 75. See the novel's final chapter for Sir Thomas's thorough self-criticism in the matter of his children's education, and his acknowledgment that he had allowed Mrs. Norris to wrest effective control from him (Ch. XLVIII, p. 465).

22 D. W. Harding, "Regulated Hatred: An Aspect of the Work of Jane Austen," *Scrutiny*, VIII (1940), 351.

iv. *The Psychology of Moral Character*

1 The psychological sources of my approach to character-structure in this chapter are too diffuse for systematic references. It will be seen that I have used Freudian, revisionist, and existential psychoanalytic concepts as they seemed locally explanatory. The only justification for my eclecticism is a perspectival one: by avoiding discipleship in any school I have tried to fuse the best insights modern psychology has to offer. References to background works used are made in the notes to the following chapter and in the Bibliography.

2 Mary Lascelles, *Jane Austen and Her Art* (Oxford, 1939), pp. 214–215.

3 "Fanny Price, agonised with jealousy, is kept waiting for her ride while Edmund is taking her rival for a turn on her horse. She does not admit she is jealous even to herself, but her irritation vents itself in a sudden spirit of indignation at the inconsiderate way they are tiring the animal. 'She began to think it rather hard upon the mare to have such double duty; if she were forgotten, the poor mare should be remembered.'

". . . Fanny is unselfish and high-minded. But Jane Austen perceives that these same virtues bring along with them, as a necessary corollary, certain weaknesses; that Fanny's very habit of self-abnegation led her, if for once she had a selfish feeling, to disguise it from herself; that her very strictness of principle was liable to make her unjust to her more frivolous rival." (David Cecil, *Jane Austen* [Cambridge, 1935], pp. 28–29.)

4 *The Rhetoric of Fiction* (Chicago and London, 1961), *passim*. See also Booth's discussion of Emma (pp. 243–266) as a "flawed" reflector comparable to Fanny, for whom the author manages to create both sympathy and judgment.

5 It has been inferred that Fanny's rejection of Portsmouth for its lack of

Notes

decorum implies an affirmation of Mansfield for having, according to Fanny, "a propriety, an attention towards every body which there was not here" (Ch. XXXVIII, p. 383). The gentry cannot be considered preferable on grounds of superior manners; Fanny's statement belies the conditions under which she had suffered for eight years. Nevertheless, the lower middle class is portrayed, in the Prices, as so burdened by its limited resources as to be unable to love. This is Fanny's main complaint: "But manner Fanny did not want. Would they but love her, she should be satisfied." (Ch. XXXVIII, p. 377.)

   6 (Columbus, Ohio, 1962.)

   7 Sheila Kaye-Smith and G. B. Stern, *Speaking of Jane Austen* (New York and London, 1944), p. 89.

v. The Structure of the Myth

   1 Duffy, *op. cit.*, pp. 75, 90, 91.

   2 Heinz L. and Rowena R. Ansbacher, eds., *The Individual Psychology of Alfred Adler* (New York, 1956), p. 53.

   3 The definitive list of these universal variants is Stith Thompson's *Motif-Index of Folk-Literature* (Helsinki and Bloomington, Ind., 1932–36), Ch. L. In analyzing this myth I have assimilated, though not imitated, the "structuralist" method of Claude Lévi-Strauss. See *Structural Anthropology*, Claire Jacobson and Brooke G. Schoepf, trans. (New York and London, 1963 [1958]), pp. 206–231. Indeed, my interest in the structuralist school of literary as well as mythic interpretation lies behind the choice of the title for this chapter. My account of the Eden motif owes much to Northrup Frye's *Anatomy of Criticism*, although it does not follow his formulations.

   4 The fullest account of the sociological content of the story is still, to my knowledge, Andrew Lang's edition of *Perrault's Popular Tales* (Oxford, 1888), Introduction to "Cendrillon: Cinderella," pp. lxxxvi–cii.

   5 Inheritance of Mansfield is also an explicit subject of discussion: Mary and Edmund are concerned with it throughout their courtship. The closest approach to an actual transfer of rights from the elder to the younger occurs with the near-fatal illness of Tom Bertram (brought on, in true fabular fashion, by excessive sowing of wild oats). Mary is quite open in wishing Tom to die and Edmund to succeed. It is possible that Edmund's revulsion when he becomes aware of his own desires in this direction encourages him to give up Mary.

   6 *The Standard Edition of the Complete Psychological Works of Sigmund Freud*, XII, 294. The quotations below are from pages 296 and 301 respectively.

   7 *Ibid.*, XVIII, 63. To clarify this sketchy summary of a profound essay, the following is useful:
"It would be in contradiction to the conservative nature of the instincts if the goal of life were a state of things which had never yet been attained. On the contrary, it must be an *old* state of things, an initial state from which the living entity has at one time or other departed and to which it is striving to return. . . . If we are to take it as a truth that knows no exception that everything living dies for *internal* reasons — becomes inorganic once again — then we shall be compelled to say that 'the aim of all life is death.' " (*Ibid.*, XVIII, 38.)

   8 *Op. cit.*, p. 230.

A Reading of *Mansfield Park*

9 What is the role of the nominal hero, Edmund, in the myth? Despite the fact that Henry is, up to the crisis, the more obvious candidate for Prince Charming, in the end Edmund reluctantly fills the role. His function is to release the heroine from her bondage by performing a repugnant deed: giving up his true love and marrying a girl he has always considered a sister — here the enchanted maiden and the unpleasant sexual partner are one and the same. Consequently, his rejecting Mary Crawford for a subsequent winning of Fanny is both the liberation of the hero and heroine and a turning from life to death.

The fairy tale structure of *Mansfield Park* is an instance of what Otto Rank has called "fairy tales of deliverance." In this pattern, the enchanted maiden is awakened from her long sleep — brought back to life — by the hero's love-inspired deeds. But in this novel, the hero's reviving the chosen one runs counter to his tendency to embrace death and withdraw from life. How can these antitheses be reconciled?

Without committing oneself to the whole of psychoanalytic doctrine about the return to the womb, one can find a way out of the difficulty in Rank's *The Trauma of Birth* (New York, 1952, pp. 106 ff.). The hero's waking the sleeper has to do with his own desire to be reborn. Birth, his own rebirth included, the hero regards ambivalently. The universal urge to return to the womb is a longing both for the extinction of consciousness and for the most thoroughgoing state of sensory bliss. Thus Edmund simultaneously chooses love and death, and his choice carries the same comic ambivalence as do other aspects of the resolution.

10 The clearest description of this ethical disturbance in Jane Austen's world is given, all too briefly, by Edwin Muir:

"Justice has never been done to Jane Austen's power of evoking a sense of evil. It is shown most vividly perhaps in 'Mansfield Park,' and in surprising circumstances. . . . The reader, from his place far outside Miss Austen's world, cannot understand the reasons for Edmund's indignation; to perform a play seems an innocent amusement. Yet as the rehearsals go on, as Mr. Crawford whispers endearments to the two Miss Bertrams, playing one against the other, as Edmund himself is involuntarily drawn in by his love for Crawford's sister, a sense of pervading evil gradually fills the scene, and the corruption of the Crawfords, only latent until then, diffuses itself over the whole company." ("Jane Austen and the Sense of Evil," *New York Times Book Review*, August 28, 1949, p. 1.)

11 The doubleness of Mansfield as the goal of all striving is summed up in a modern syncretist's description of the World-Navel, the goal of heroic quest in widespread mythologies: ". . . since it is the source of all existence, it yields the world's plenitude of both good and evil. Ugliness and beauty, sin and virtue, pleasure and pain, are equally its production." (Joseph Campbell, *The Hero with a Thousand Faces*, New York, 1956 [1949], p. 44.)

12 C. G. Jung, *The Archetypes and the Collective Unconscious*, R. F. C. Hull, trans. (New York and London, 1959), p. 164. Fanny's peculiar mixture of fragility and potency may seem inexplicable or unreal, unless we take into account another statement of Jung's:

"It is a striking paradox in all child myths that the 'child' is on the one hand delivered helpless into the power of terrible enemies and in continual danger of extinction, while on the other he possesses powers far exceeding those of ordinary humanity. This is closely related to the psychological fact that

Notes

though the child may be 'insignificant,' unknown, 'a mere child,' he is also divine. . . . [The 'child' symbol] is a personification of vital forces quite outside the limited range of our conscious mind; of ways and possibilities of which our one-sided conscious mind knows nothing; a wholeness which embraces the very depths of Nature. It represents the strongest, the most ineluctable urge in every being, namely the urge to realize itself." (P. 170.)

Since Fanny probably fails to achieve this kind of wholeness, we may think her a poor example of this tradition. But if we regard the duality of incompetence and fulfillment as a dynamic process rather than a static contradiction we can see Fanny's career as just this "urge" from helplessness and inchoateness of personality to self-definition and mastery of her world.

VI. *The Novel and Its Tradition*

1 The Macdonald Illustrated Classics edition (London, 1957). Quotations are from pp. vii, xiv, xiv–xv, xv, and xii respectively. Additional remarks of interest: ". . . what we are offered is a parable, something that no English novelist had attempted before" (p. xv); ". . . *Mansfield Park*, alone of the Austen novels, is tragic (in spite of the appearance of a happy ending)" (p. xvii).

2 Lionel Trilling, *E. M. Forster* (Norfolk, Conn., 1943), p. 118.

3 *Howards End* (New York, 1954 [1910]), p. 187.

4 Both novels also take up the gentry as colonialists, the later one developing the anticipations of the earlier. Forster considers the modern colonist "a super-yeoman, who carries his country's virtue overseas. But the Imperialist is not what he thinks or seems. He is a destroyer. He prepares the way for cosmopolitanism, and though his ambitions may be fulfilled, the earth that he inherits will be grey." (*Ibid.*, p. 323.)

5 See Trilling, *op. cit.*, p. 134, for the Faust symbolism in *Howards End*.

6 *Jane Austen and Her Art*, p. 164.

7 Reuben A. Brower, "The Controlling Hand: Jane Austen and 'Pride and Prejudice,'" *Scrutiny*, XIII (1945), 111.

8 Ian Watt, *The Rise of the Novel: Studies in Defoe, Richardson, and Fielding* (Harmondsworth, England, 1963 [1957]), pp. 308–311, provides an excellent summary of her place in the development of realism: "Jane Austen's novels, in short, must be seen as the most successful solutions of the two general narrative problems for which Richardson and Fielding had provided only partial answers. She was able to combine into a harmonious unity the advantages both of realism of presentation and realism of assessment, of the internal and of the external approaches to character." (P. 310.)

9 See Sartre's discussion of being for others (*être-pour-autrui*) in Part III of *L'être et le néant*. This has been translated as *Being and Nothingness: An Essay on Phenomenological Ontology*, Hazel E. Barnes, trans. (New York, 1956).

10 See Lionel Trilling, "On the Teaching of Modern Literature," in *Beyond Culture: Essays on Literature and Learning* (New York, 1965), which also contains an important article on *Emma*.

BIBLIOGRAPHY

Bibliography

This list — exhaustive neither of published works nor of works used in this study — is divided into sections roughly corresponding to the chapters of the text, to indicate each title's main, but not exclusive, relevance.

I. Texts, Bibliographies, Textual Studies

Austen, Jane. *Letters to Her Sister Cassandra and Others.* 2 vols. R. W. Chapman, ed. Oxford, 1932.
—————. *The Novels of Jane Austen.* 5 vols. Oxford, 1948 [1923]. Vol. III: *Mansfield Park.* This text is also available in the Riverside edition, with an introduction by Reuben A. Brower.
—————. *Plan of a Novel according to Hints from Various Quarters, with Opinions on Mansfield Park and Emma.* Oxford, 1926.
—————. *Lady Susan* and *The Watsons.* New York, 1931 [1871].
Austen-Leigh, William, and Richard Arthur Austen-Leigh. *Jane Austen: Her Life and Letters: A Family Record.* New York, 1913.
Chapman, R. W. *Jane Austen: Facts and Problems.* Oxford, 1949 [1948].
—————. *Jane Austen, A Critical Bibliography.* Oxford, 1953.
Keynes, Geoffrey. *Jane Austen: A Bibliography.* London, 1929.
Leavis, Q. D. "A Critical Theory of Jane Austen's Writings," and "*Lady Susan* into *Mansfield Park,*" *Scrutiny,* X (1942), nos. 1, 2, 3. See also her introduction to the Macdonald edition of *Mansfield Park,* London, 1957.

II. Criticism, Especially with Reference to Mansfield Park

Amis, Kingsley. "What Became of Jane Austen? *Mansfield Park.*" *Spectator,* CIC (1957), 339–340.
Babb, Howard S. *Jane Austen's Novels: The Fabric of Dialogue.* N.p. [Columbus, Ohio], 1962.

A Reading of *Mansfield Park*

Bradbrook, Frank W. "Sources of Jane Austen's Ideas about Nature in 'Mansfield Park.'" *Notes and Queries*, n.s., CCVI (1961), 222–224.

Bradley, A. C. "Jane Austen." *Essays and Studies*, II (1911).

Branton, Clarence L. "The Ordinations in Jane Austen's Novels." *Nineteenth-Century Fiction*, X (1955–56), 156–159.

Brower, Reuben A. "The Controlling Hand: Jane Austen and 'Pride and Prejudice.'" *Scrutiny*, XIII (1945), 99–111.

Cecil, Lord David. *Jane Austen*. Cambridge, 1935.

Chapman, R. W. "Jane Austen and Crabbe." *Times Literary Supplement*, April 7, 1927, p. 251.

Collins, Barbara B. "Jane Austen's Victorian Novel." *Nineteenth-Century Fiction*, IV (1949), 175–185.

Craik, W. A. *Jane Austen: The Six Novels*. London, 1965.

Daiches, David. "Jane Austen, Karl Marx, and the Aristocratic Dance." *American Scholar*, XVII (1947–48), 289–296.

Donohue, Joseph W., Jr. "Ordination and the Divided House at Mansfield Park." *ELH*, XXXII (1965), 169–178.

Duffy, James M., Jr. "Moral Integrity and Moral Anarchy in *Mansfield Park*." *ELH*, XXII (1956), 71–91.

Edwards, Thomas R., Jr. "The Difficult Beauty of *Mansfield Park*." *Nineteenth-Century Fiction*, XX (1965), 51–67.

Farrer, Reginald. "Jane Austen: ob., July 18, 1817." *The Quarterly Review*, CCXXVIII (1917), 1–30.

Garrod, H. W. "Jane Austen: A Depreciation." *Essays by Divers Hands*, n.s., VIII (1928), 21–40.

Greene, Donald J. "Jane Austen and the Peerage." *PMLA*, LXVIII (1953), 1017–1031.

Harding, D. W. "Regulated Hatred: An Aspect of the Work of Jane Austen." *Scrutiny*, VIII (1940), 346–362.

Hogan, Charles Beecher. "Jane Austen and Her Early Public." *Review of English Studies*, n.s., I (1950), 39–54.

Kaye-Smith, Sheila, and G. B. Stern. *More about Jane Austen*. New York and London, 1949.

————. *Speaking of Jane Austen*. New York and London, 1944.

Kettle, Arnold. *An Introduction to the English Novel*. 2 vols. New York and Evanston, 1960 [1951].

Lascelles, Mary. *Jane Austen and Her Art*. Oxford, 1939.

————. "Some Characteristics of Jane Austen's Style." *Essays and Studies*, XXII (1937), 61–85.

Litz, A. Walton. *Jane Austen: A Study of Her Artistic Development*. New York, 1965.

Meyerstein, E. H. W. "Crabbe and 'Mansfield Park.'" *Times Literary Supplement*, March 31, 1927, p. 232.

Mudrick, Marvin. *Jane Austen: Irony as Defense and Discovery*. Princeton, 1952. Ch. VI: "The Triumph of Gentility: *Mansfield Park*."

Muir, Edwin. "Jane Austen and the Sense of Evil." *The New York Times Book Review*, August 28, 1949, pp. 1, 25.

Murrah, Charles. "The Background of *Mansfield Park*." In *From Jane Austen to Joseph Conrad*, Robert C. Rathburn and Martin Steinmann, Jr., eds. Minneapolis, 1958, pp. 23–34.

Bibliography

Parks, Edd Winfield. "Exegesis in Jane Austen's Novels." *South Atlantic Quarterly*, LI (1952), 103–119.

Trilling, Lionel. "A Portrait of Western Man." *Listener*, XLIX (1953), 969 ff.

————. "*Mansfield Park*." *Partisan Review*, XXI (1954), 492–511. Reprinted in *The Opposing Self: Nine Essays in Criticism*, New York, 1955.

Woolf, Leonard. "The Economic Determinism of Jane Austen." *New Statesman and Nation*, n.s., XXIV (1942), pp. 39–41.

Wright, Andrew H. *Jane Austen's Novels: A Study in Structure*, London, 1953.

IIIa. *Political, Economic, and Social History*

Brailsford, H. N. *Shelley, Godwin, and Their Circle.* New York and London, n.d.

Brinton, Crane. *The Political Ideas of the English Romanticists.* London, etc., 1926.

Brown, Ford K. *Fathers of the Victorians: The Age of Wilberforce.* Cambridge, 1961.

Burn, W. J. *The British West Indies.* London, etc., 1951.

Drummond, Andrew L. *The Churches in English Fiction,* Leicester, 1950.

Gregory, Allene. *The French Revolution and the English Novel.* New York and London, 1915.

Halévy, Elie. *A History of the English People in the Nineteenth Century.* 6 vols. E. I. Watkin and D. A. Barker, trans. New York, 1961 [1913 ff.]. Vol. I, *England in 1815.*

MacLean, Kenneth. *Agrarian Age: A Background for Wordsworth.* New Haven and London, 1951.

Mingay, G. E. *English Landed Society in the Eighteenth Century.* London and Toronto, 1963.

Ragatz, L. J. *The Fall of the Planter Class in the British Caribbean, 1763–1833: A Study in Social and Economic History.* New York and London, 1928.

Spring, David. "Aristocracy, Social Structure, and Religion in the Early Victorian Period." *Victorian Studies*, VI (1962–63), 263–280.

Thompson, F. M. L. *English Landed Society in the Nineteenth Century.* London and Toronto, 1963.

Warner, Oliver. *William Wilberforce and His Times.* London, 1962.

Warner, Wellman J. *The Wesleyan Movement and the Industrial Revolution,* London, New York, and Toronto, 1930.

IIIb. *The Theatricals and Their Background*

Butler, E. M. "Mansfield Park and Kotzebue's 'Lovers' Vows.'" *Modern Language Review*, XXVIII (1933), 326–327.

Hazlitt. *The Collected Works of William Hazlitt.* 12 vols. A. R. Waller and Arnold Glover, eds. London and New York, 1902. Vol. V.

Husbands, H. Winifred. "'Mansfield Park' and 'Lovers' Vows': A Reply." *Modern Language Review*, XXIX (1934), 176 ff.

Inchbald, Elizabeth, ed. *The British Theatre: or, A Collection of Plays . . .,* 25 vols. London, 1808. Vols. XVI, XXIII.

Lodge, David. "A Question of Judgment: The Theatricals at Mansfield Park." *Nineteenth-Century Fiction*, XVII (1962), 275–282.

A Reading of *Mansfield Park*

Nicoll, Allardyce. *A History of Late Eighteenth Century Drama: 1750–1800*, Cambridge, 1927.

Pink, M. Alderton. "Jane Austen and a Forgotten Dramatist." *The Nineteenth Century and After*, CII (1927), 125–134.

Reitzel, William. "*Mansfield Park* and *Lovers' Vows*." *Review of English Studies*, IX (1933), 451–456.

Rosenfeld, Sybil. "Jane Austen and Private Theatricals." *Essays and Studies*, 1962, pp. 40–51.

Tunney, Hubert J., ed. "*Home's Douglas*." *Bulletin of the University of Kansas Humanistic Studies*, III (1924), 129–228.

Wordsworth. *The Poetical Works of William Wordsworth*. E. De Selincourt, ed. Oxford, 1952 [1944]. Vol. II.

iv, v. *Psychology and Mythology*

Adler. *The Individual Psychology of Alfred Adler*. Heinz L. and Rowena R. Ansbacher, eds. New York, 1956.

Campbell, Joseph. *The Hero with a Thousand Faces*. New York, 1956 [1949].

Freud. *The Standard Edition of the Complete Psychological Works of Sigmund Freud*. James Strachey *et al.*, trans. London, 1958. Vols. IX, XII, XVIII.

Jones, Ernest. *Essays in Applied Psychoanalysis*. Vol. II: *Essays in Folklore, Anthropology and Religion*. London, 1951.

Jung. *The Collected Works of C. G. Jung*. Herbert Read, Michael Fordham, and Gerhard Adler, eds., 17+ vols. Vol. 9, Part 1: *The Archetypes and the Collective Unconscious*, R. F. C. Hull, trans. London and New York, 1959.

Lang, Andrew, ed. *Perrault's Popular Tales*. Oxford, 1888.

Lévi-Strauss, Claude. *Structural Anthropology*. Claire Jacobson and Brooke G. Schoepf, trans. New York and London, 1963 [1958].

May, Rollo. Ernest Angel and Henri F. Ellenberger, eds. *Existence: A New Dimension in Psychiatry and Psychology*. New York, 1958.

Rank, Otto. *The Trauma of Birth*. New York, 1952.

Ruitenbeek, Hendrik M., ed. *Psychoanalysis and Existential Philosophy*. New York, 1962.

Sartre, Jean-Paul. *Being and Nothingness: An Essay on Phenomenological Ontology*. Hazel E. Barnes, trans. New York, 1956.

Thompson, Stith. *Motif-Index of Folk-Literature*. 6 vols. *Folklore Fellows Communications*. Helsinki, 1932–36. Vol. XLVI, no. 116. Also published as *Indiana University Studies*. Bloomington, Ind., Vol. XXI, no. 108.

vi. *Literary Relationships*

Booth, Wayne. *The Rhetoric of Fiction*. Chicago and London, 1961.

Forster, E. M. *Abinger Harvest*. London, 1942. ("Jane, How Shall We Ever Recollect . . .")

_____. *Aspects of the Novel*. New York, 1927.

_____. *Howards End*. New York, 1954 [1910].

Harvey, W. J. *Character and the Novel*. Ithaca, N.Y., 1965.

Leavis, F. R. *The Great Tradition*. New York, 1954 [1948].

Lukacs, Georg. *Studies in European Realism*. New York, 1964.

Bibliography

Ortega y Gasset, José. *The Dehumanization of Art and Other Writings on Art and Culture.* Garden City, N.Y., 1956.

Trilling, Lionel. *E. M. Forster.* Norfolk, Conn., 1943.

————. *Beyond Culture: Essays on Literature and Learning.* New York, 1965.

Watt, Ian. *The Rise of the Novel: Studies in Defoe, Richardson, and Fielding.* Harmondsworth, England, 1963 [1957].

INDEX

Index

Index